Reading Argumentative Texts

Reading Argumentative Texts

Analytic Tools to Improve Understanding

James E. Scheuermann

ROWMAN & LITTLEFIELD
Lanham • Boulder • New York • London

Published by Rowman & Littlefield
An imprint of The Rowman & Littlefield Publishing Group, Inc.
4501 Forbes Boulevard, Suite 200, Lanham, Maryland 20706
www.rowman.com

86-90 Paul Street, London EC2A 4NE, United Kingdom

Copyright © 2022 by James E. Scheuermann

All rights reserved. No part of this book may be reproduced in any form or by any electronic or mechanical means, including information storage and retrieval systems, without written permission from the publisher, except by a reviewer who may quote passages in a review.

British Library Cataloguing in Publication Information Available

Library of Congress Cataloging-in-Publication Data Available

ISBN 9781475864526 (cloth) | ISBN 9781475864533 (pbk.)
 | ISBN 9781475864540 (ebook)

To the memory of my parents, Otto and Frances Scheuermann, whose love and many sacrifices can never be repaid, only acknowledged and passed to the next generation by works such as this.

Contents

Preface	ix
Acknowledgments	xiii
Chapter 1: Introduction	1
Chapter 2: Reading Is Not a Spectator Sport	15
Chapter 3: Why Are You Reading?	23
Chapter 4: Arguments: A Closer Look	31
Chapter 5: Every Person Has a Skeleton, Every Argument Has a Structure	53
Chapter 6: What Does the Skeleton Look Like? Outlines and Summaries	73
Chapter 7: Ambiguity and Nonliteral Uses of Language	93
Chapter 8: Context Imparts Meaning	111
Chapter 9: The ABCs of Logic	119
Chapter 10: Conclusion	135
Appendix A: Study Latin If You Want to Talk Like a Supervillain *Frankie Thomas*	137

Appendix B: Ayanna Pressley Is Right: 16-Year-Olds Deserve the
    Right to Vote   139
    Nancy Deutsch

Index   143

About the Author   145

Preface

This book is an introduction to acquiring and mastering tools you can use to better understand the meaning of nonfiction, argumentative texts. These texts include editorials in newspapers, magazines, and internet websites; articles, essays, and books in various academic fields (history, philosophy, political science, psychology, sociology); and printed speeches, sermons, and lectures.

The meaning of an argumentative text is to be found in the argument that the text articulates and in the other parts of the text that are not part of the argument. These other parts may illuminate or obscure the meaning of the argument, emphasize or de-emphasize certain parts of the argument, make the argument more or less persuasive, or be irrelevant to the argument. Accordingly, while this book focuses on the analysis and understanding of argumentative texts, it is not limited to the analysis of arguments, argument-types, or errors in argumentation (fallacies), although it does discuss each of these topics.

The principal sources of the meaning of an argumentative text we examine here include:

1. the structure of the text—and so we will examine various types of introductions and the benefits of outlining and summarizing
2. key sentences, phrases, and words in a text—so we discuss ambiguity, the difference between factual and normative statements, irony, and rhetoric
3. context—specifically, intellectual, social, political, cultural, and physical context, and
4. the logical connections between terms in an argument, including fallacies and the distinction between necessary and sufficient conditions.

These sources of meaning are illustrated through numerous examples (including complete essays) and occasional invitations for the reader to employ one of the analytical tools under discussion before reading how I use that tool to analyze a text. These sources are further analyzed through exercises and case studies found in the companion book, *A Workbook for Reading Argumentative Texts*. While *Reading Argumentative Texts* is entirely self-contained and instructive as a stand-alone textbook, its use in conjunction with *Workbook* provides a more in-depth course of study of the tools presented here.

As an introduction, this book discusses only the essential tools of analyzing argumentative texts. A more comprehensive guide could easily be several times the length of this work. A much longer book may also be, as a result, less accessible and of less utility to many students and their instructors who need to learn the fundamentals of analyzing argumentative texts in a course that also is designed to teach critical thinking, rhetoric, or writing.

If you are a student in a college or university struggling to make sense of the many articles and books that you have been assigned to read, this book is for you. I was once in your position, and I know that the work involved in making sense of a mountain of new texts can be overwhelming. I have written this book to give you the most useful and practical tools many people have learned over the years that will allow you to make sense of those texts, to get past a superficial understanding of them, and to take a deep dive into their richness of meaning. Being able to understand argumentative texts will enrich and change your life for the better.

If you are a student in or professor of a critical thinking course, this book is for you. Whether used in conjunction with the accompanying *Workbook* or not, it can be used as the sole, principal, or supplementary textbook in a critical thinking course. This book provides the essential tools for critical thinking (as that term is used in numerous courses in higher education). It is guided by the principle that the heart of critical thinking is the analysis of a text to understand an author's meaning. Critical thinking is fundamentally analytical thinking. Once a reader understands an author's meaning and how she communicates it, the reader is then in a position to offer a thoughtful assessment of the merits and weaknesses of the author's argument. Without real understanding of the meaning of a text, any such assessment ("criticism" in the more colloquial sense) is of little value.

If you are a student in or professor of a rhetoric course, this book is for you. Because this book is premised on the view that the meaning of an argumentative text is to be found in the argument and in the nonargumentative parts of the text, it devotes substantial effort to distinguishing the argumentative and the rhetorical parts of texts. These discussions illuminate and illustrate the nature of arguments and of rhetorical appeals, the difference between them, and how they may both be employed in communicating meaning to an audience. If you pick up a rhetoric textbook published before 1970, you may well find a discussion of certain of the tools and concepts presented in this book. That speaks both to the plasticity of the term "rhetoric" and of the long-recognized need for students to become improved readers through their mastery of the tools discussed here.

If you are a student in higher education taking a writing course, here's an important fact that will help you succeed in that course: being a better writer and being a better reader are two sides of the same coin. To use a different metaphor, writers and readers are two voices in the same dialogue, a dialogue between a teacher (the author) and a learner (the reader). The tools I present in this book are tools for better reading and, with a change in perspective, tools to improve your writing as well. So, if you want to be a better writer of the nonfiction term papers or essays you have been assigned, this book is for you.

By the same token, if you are a teacher of one of those writing courses, this book is for you and your students. Many of the standard writing texts for entry-level writing courses do not touch on reading argumentative texts or do so only in a chapter or two. Because better readers are better writers, a more extended and deeper study of reading skills should foster better outcomes for your students. For those instructors who have not offered such extended and deeper study for lack of an appropriate course book, your search is over. This book is relatively short, and so can be integrated with one or more other textbooks in your course. It is written in a nontechnical, conversational style. That means that you do not need to spend time explaining numerous terms of art from the social sciences or communication theories before you teach the practical tools your students need to better understand argumentative texts. It also means that your students can more readily and immediately learn those practical tools.

However you describe yourself and wherever you are in your educational journey, you can improve your understanding of what you read. Learning how to read well and specifically learning to read for greater understanding of argumentative texts, are skills that are infinitely perfectible. Thankfully, the effort involved has many rewards.

I wrote this book to give voice and effect to two beliefs. The first is that each of us can get a lot better at understanding argumentative texts. The second is that a person who cannot analyze and understand argumentative texts is always at a disadvantage in their work and in many essential aspects of their personal, social, cultural, and political life. The first belief implies that none of us *has* to be a person with underdeveloped reading skills. The second belief teaches that if your reading skills are below par, you will miss a lot of the meaning and richness life has to offer. And you will have less power over your life than does someone who has acquired these skills. That is a real loss—for you and for all of us as a community. Each of us gets only one life to live. Better that it is a rich and full life, a life of flourishing, an empowered life.

Reflect for a moment on how thin, how threadbare, your life would be if you had no shared sense of meaning with others. That shared meaning may come from a common appreciation of a form of art (hip-hop, ballet, Rodin's sculptures), a similar sense of humor, loyalty to a basketball team, affiliation with a school or club, common religious beliefs, or some other source. Reading an argumentative text to understand what the author meant creates shared meaning, between you and the author and, in turn, between you and those with whom you share this understanding. That shared meaning creates stronger social relations, stronger community bonds, and enriches and empowers the lives that embrace it. Lives like yours.

The cliché that "teachers often learn from their students" is an old cliché because it is true. I am no different. I welcome any comments you have on this book—the parts you found most useful, how to make the book more useful, the parts that are too difficult or too easy, anything you think I should add, and so on. You can email your comments to me at analyzingtexts@gmail.com.

Acknowledgments

In the course of writing and rewriting the many drafts of this book, I have had the benefit of the thoughtful commentary and criticisms of many friends, former colleagues, and associates. I owe each of them a special thanks and debt of gratitude. I want to mention particularly Bruno F. Battistoli, PhD, formerly Assistant Professor of Communication and Coordinator of Television and Radio Programs at Fairleigh Dickinson University, who provided extensive written and oral comments on three chapters of the manuscript. I am fortunate that he has brought his good judgment to bear on this project. He has been a friend for more than 30 years and is a person of constant good cheer. I have no doubt that he will be forgiving of my resistance to many of his suggestions for improvement.

Other readers and commentators include, in alphabetical order: Ernest Alleva, PhD, Associate Dean for Academic Support and Advising and Senior Faculty Associate, Humanities and Arts at Hampshire College; Neal James Corbelli; Christina Fisanick, PhD, Associate Professor of English, California University of Pennsylvania; John Lawson, PhD, Professor of English, Robert Morris University; Ailsa McCulloch; Zoe Phares; Anne M. Scheuermann (who proved that even a sibling can provide valuable advice); Charles Shanabruch, PhD, Associate Professor Emeritus of Business and formerly Dean of the Graham School of Management, St. Xavier University; John Tryneski, former Executive Editor at the University of Chicago Press; and Cynthia Weisfield.

Notwithstanding the mass of education, common sense, good judgment, and intellect brought to this project by these readers and commentators, I did not accept all of their suggestions in whole or in part. So, in the final analysis, I alone am responsible for any errors or omissions in the text.

My thanks as well to Natalie Behrends and Andrew Mullins, who provided research assistance early in my writing of this book. Natalie also offered helpful suggestions on the types of readings that readers of this book may find most interesting. Sara Camilli graciously provided her insights into the world of academic publishing.

Final thanks go to Sharon Fatur and Renee Gestrich, each of whom provided invaluable administrative assistance on drafts of the manuscript, and to Leslie Keros, who contributed her valuable skills in getting the manuscript into final form. Their patience with my limited word processing abilities is most appreciated.

CREDITS

Frankie Thomas, "Study Latin If You Want to Talk Like a supervillain," appears with the kind permission of the author, and under license; it first appeared on April 11, 2018, on the PBS *NewsHour.*

Nancy Deutsch, "Ayanna Pressley Is Right: 16-Year-Olds Deserve the Right to Vote," is reprinted under a license from *Newsweek* and the Enveritas Group, Inc.

Chapter 1

Introduction

> *Sometimes I think heaven must be one continuous unexhausted reading.—*
> Virginia Woolf (British novelist and essayist, 1882–1941), in a letter to Ethel Smyth, July 1934

> *I have always imagined that Paradise will be some kind of library.—*
> Jorge Luis Borges (Argentinian short-story writer, poet, and essayist, 1899–1986)

Imagine that you are sitting on a park bench on a hot, humid summer afternoon, not a cloud in the sky, and with time to kill. You text a friend complaining about how miserable and uncomfortable you are. Your friend texts back this message:

> Dude, it's summer. It's hot and humid—news flash. You want to cool off. Eat some ice cream. You'll feel like an April day, like springtime. The store's across the street from you. They have Cosmic Mix, your favorite flavor. If you want to try something new, go for Cherry Berry, my favorite.

So, what does this simple eight-sentence text mean? What does your friend intend to communicate to you? Is your friend making an argument? If she is making an argument, what is it? If your friend is making an argument, is she also trying to communicate something in addition to that argument? If there are statements in her text that are not part of her argument, why did she include them? If only some of the sentences state the argument, what meaning is communicated by the other sentences? Do those other sentences inform or illuminate the argument (show more clearly that the premises lead to the conclusion), obscure the argument (weaken the support the premises provide for the conclusion), have no bearing on the argument, make purely emotional appeals, or some mix of these?

These questions are what this book is all about. If you are puzzled by all or some of these questions, that is not a problem. By the time you have read this book, they will seem like old friends. We are going to discuss tools that will allow you to better analyze and, in turn, to better understand any text that is making, or may be making, an argument. Let's begin by examining your friend's text more closely to illustrate what you will learn here.

ARGUMENTS AND THE WRITINGS THAT MAKE THEM

You will not get far in answering the question whether your friend has texted you an argument unless you understand what an argument is. So, let's start there. "Argue" and "argument" sometimes refer to verbal conflict, fighting with words, contradiction, or quarrel, especially an emotional one. Your friend did not argue with you in any of those senses. She is not fighting with you in her text. That sense of "argue" is *not* what we are concerned with in this book.

Rather, for our purposes, "*argument*" is defined as:

> *the form of reasoning that states a conclusion (or thesis) and attempts to show that it is true based on the truth of one or more other related statements, which are the premise or premises.*

In other words, any time an author asserts an argument in this sense, she is saying this to her readers: *"if these statements (the premises) are true, then this statement (the conclusion) is also true"* or, *"if you know that the premises are true (and I am telling you that they are), then you know that the conclusion is true."*

In our ice cream example, your friend did make an argument. She is asserting one or more premises and stating that a conclusion follows from them. We can restate her argument, like this:

> On a hot, humid day, a person who eats ice cream will cool off. [Premise]
> It's a hot, humid day. [Premise]
> You want to cool off. [Premise]
> Therefore, eat some ice cream (or, you should eat some ice cream). [Conclusion]

The first three sentences of this argument are the premises and the last sentence is the conclusion (or thesis). The premises are the reasons on which the conclusion is based; they are what compels you to accept the conclusion.

Introduction 3

This argument, it is worth noting, is found solely in sentences two (everything before the dash), three, and four of your friend's text.

Now, if this is your friend's argument, and if the purpose of her text was to get you to eat ice cream, then all of the other sentences in her text would appear to be irrelevant to establishing her conclusion that you should eat ice cream. If they are irrelevant, why did your friend include these other sentences in her text? What did she mean by them and how do they relate to her argument, if they do? Once we press the answers to these questions, are we so sure that these other sentences are not relevant to the conclusion your friend is trying to establish?

A good place to start answering these questions is with this sentence, "The store's across the street from you." What does your friend mean by that? If you both know that you can look across the street to see the ice cream store, it is very likely that she does not intend to communicate what you already know. So, what does she mean?

A good assumption is that she intends the statement to mean what the words literally say, and that she means something else as well. That "something else" that your friend also means and intends to communicate, may be this—"it will not be any trouble or risk for you to walk to the store to buy the ice cream." And suppose that is right. Suppose the "street" is a quiet, two-lane street, lightly traveled at this time of day, and the traffic is no threat to your life and limb. Then the sentence, "The store's across the street from you," is relevant to the argument. Indeed, it is part of the argument, which we can restate like this:

On a hot, humid day, a person who eats ice cream will cool off. [Premise]
It's a hot, humid day. [Premise]
You want to cool off. [Premise]
The closest ice cream store is across a quiet, two-lane street that is lightly traveled at this time. [Premise]
Trying to cross this street will be no trouble (no inconvenience and no risk). [Premise]
Therefore, go eat some ice cream (or, you should go eat some ice cream). [Conclusion]

On this reading, your friend intends the statement, "The store's across the street from you," to provide additional support for the directive that you should go eat ice cream at the ice cream store.

But what if the facts are different? Suppose your friend is right that the ice cream store is "across the street from you," but you both also know that the "street" is a six-lane boulevard that has no traffic signals, is very busy, and has a forty-mile-per-hour speed limit. Trying to cross it for any reason could cost you your life, and risking your life for an ice cream cone may not be the most prudent thing to do.

Let's suppose further that that is a minor consideration for your friend. She is an intense person when it comes to ice cream, and especially about eating ice cream on hot summer days. She really thinks that you should eat ice cream at any risk. If that is right, then, again, she intends "The store's across the street from you" to be taken literally, but she also intends it to have additional meaning—eating ice cream is worth the risk you face in getting it. If so, then we can restate her argument like this:

> On a hot, humid day, a person who eats ice cream will cool off. [Premise]
> It's a hot, humid day. [Premise]
> You want to cool off. [Premise]
> The closest ice cream store is across a six-lane boulevard that has no traffic signals, is very busy, and has a forty-mile-per-hour speed limit. [Premise]
> Trying to cross this boulevard could cost you your life. [Premise]
> Eating ice cream now is worth the risk. [Premise]
> Therefore, (you should) go eat ice cream. [Conclusion]

Once again, the sentence "The store's across the street from you" is part of the argument, but now she is communicating something very different by that sentence than she was communicating when we supposed that she knew the street to be a quiet, two-lane street.

Now, consider this part of her text:

> You'll feel like an April day, like springtime. . . . They have Cosmic Mix, your favorite. If you want to try something new, go for Cherry Berry, my favorite.

At first glance, these sentences do not appear to be relevant to your friend's argument that you should eat ice cream to cool off. So, why has your friend included them in her text?

Maybe she knows that you are not usually moved to action by a purely logical argument like this—"ice cream will cool you off; you want to be cooled off; so, go eat some ice cream." She knows that you usually need to have a logical argument wrapped in a pretty verbal package before you will act as logic alone demands. In that case, in addition to her purely logical argument, she is trying to persuade you to act in a manner consistent with her directive ("eat ice cream" or "you should eat ice cream") by appealing to your emotions and feelings ("Oh, if I could feel like springtime, with cool April temperatures"), and to your nonrational tastes ("there's no ice cream better than Cosmic Mix"), and to your appreciation of her tastes in food ("she likes Cherry Berry, and she has good taste").

On this interpretation of these sentences, your friend's text contains an argument and several other sentences that strictly are not part of her argument as she intends to make it, but rather are designed to persuade you to act as her argument directs. In other words, these sentences are rhetorical; they are designed to persuade you to act based on appeals to your emotions, feelings, or shared values, or by appeal to the credibility or reputation of the writer. We will discuss rhetorical statements further in chapters 4 and 7.

Finally, let's take a closer look at the sentence, "You'll feel like an April day, like springtime." Maybe that is not part of the argument that ice cream will cool you down and it is just an appeal to your emotions and feelings. Consider, however, whether there is an interpretation of it that makes it part of the argument.

Suppose your friend's text did not have that sentence. Then when you read her text you may ask yourself, "Well, will ice cream cool me down a lot, enough to make a real difference? Because if it doesn't, I'm not going to trouble myself to cross the street and buy ice cream." By including her "April day, like springtime" sentence, she may be trying to answer that implied question. She may intend to give greater meaning to the sentence, "You want to cool off" and specifically, to the phrase, "cool off." Specifically, she may intend the reference to April and springtime to communicate that you will cool off so much that you are no longer uncomfortable.

In that case, then, she intends a more factual (and less figurative) restatement of the sentence "You'll feel like an April day, like springtime" to be part of her argument. That more factual restatement would be something like this, "Eating ice cream will cool you off to a comfortable temperature, and not just a little," and her argument would be stated like this:

On a hot, humid day, a person who eats ice cream will cool off. [Premise]
It's a hot, humid day. [Premise]
You want to cool off. [Premise]
Eating ice cream will cool you off to a comfortable temperature, and not just a little. [Premise]
Therefore, eat some ice cream (or, you should eat some ice cream). [Conclusion]

She intends the sentence comparing eating ice cream to April and springtime to give greater meaning to her argument by giving additional meaning and clarity to the vague phrase "cool off."

We do not need to decide which of these alternative interpretations is better, or to examine whether there are still other reasonable interpretations of this text. It is enough to note here that there is an essential conclusion to be drawn from this ice cream example. Before we get to that, however, it will be productive to consider a different type of argument and a couple of examples.

The ice cream argument is intended to be a "*practical*" argument in the sense that it is intended to be action-guiding. Your friend is directing you to do something, "eat ice cream." Imperative sentences, like this one, are not true or false. Rather, they are commands to do something. An imperative sentence, however, can be restated as a declarative "ought" or "should" or "must" sentence that can be thought of as true or false. Here, that declarative sentence is, "you should (or ought to or must) eat ice cream." We will look at many other practical arguments later in this book.

Other arguments are not intended to be practical in this sense, but rather are intended to confirm a conclusion that has no direct connection to anyone's doing anything. They are generally called theoretical arguments, where "*theoretical*" just means "not action-guiding." The conclusion of a "theoretical" argument can state a fact (my dog has four legs), an opinion ("Adele has a beautiful voice"), or a theoretical point (in Sir Isaac Newton's theory of physics, "force equals mass times acceleration").[1] Here's a very simple theoretical argument, from ancient Athens, more than 2000 years ago:

All men are mortal. [Premise]
Socrates is a man. [Premise]
Therefore, Socrates is mortal. [Conclusion]

The conclusion is obvious, of course. This argument is nonetheless theoretical in that it does not tell anyone to do something.

Here is a passage that contains a theoretical argument that is timelier and more serious:

Since 1970, the population of birds in North America has declined by three billion, which is a loss of nearly one-third of the bird population. Robust bird populations indicate a healthy ecosystem. Massive losses of birds indicate an ecosystem in dire trouble. We conclude that our North American ecosystem is not healthy and is in real trouble.[2]

To put this in the form of an argument:

Since 1970, the population of birds in North America has declined by three billion, which is a loss of nearly one-third of the bird population. [Premise]
This is a massive loss of the bird population. [Premise]

A massive loss of a bird population indicates an ecosystem in dire trouble. [Premise]
Therefore, our North American ecosystem is in dire trouble (not healthy). [Conclusion]

This argument does not direct any person or entity to do anything. It simply states the fact or opinion that our North American ecosystem is in dire trouble. In that sense, it is a theoretical argument.

There is a lot to chew on just from these few examples of texts making arguments about ice cream, Socrates, and bird populations. In this book we will consider many, diverse argumentative texts, some dealing with relatively trivial topics (like our examples about ice cream and Socrates) and some more serious. Before we move on, however, what lesson is to be drawn from the examples of arguments we have discussed so far?

The lesson (the tool for your reading toolbox) is this: virtually every writing that makes an argument will have some sentences that are part of the argument itself and other sentences that give key terms in the argument additional meaning or obscure that meaning, that make parts of the argument more or less persuasive, that are only indirectly related to the argument, or that are not relevant to the argument. More generally, *the meaning of an argumentative text is the thoughts and emotions the author intends to communicate. That meaning is found not only in (1) the statements that constitute the argument but also in (2) the statements that are not part of the argument and (3) the relations between the argumentative statements themselves and between those statements and the nonargumentative parts.* Understanding the meaning of an argumentative work is a matter of understanding the argument itself and the other parts of the intellectual stew of which it is a part.

PURPOSE AND METHOD: WHERE ARE WE GOING AND HOW ARE WE GOING TO GET THERE?

You read in the Preface that the purpose of this book is to provide you with tools to become a better reader of nonfiction, argumentative texts. That may seem fairly straightforward. But what does this sentence mean? What is a "text," an "argumentative text," a "better reader"?

For our purposes, a *"text"* is any written or printed work that is the product of human thought, as contrasted to random scribblings. You already know what an *"argument"* is. We defined that term earlier as: the form of reasoning that states a conclusion (or thesis) and attempts to show that it is true based on the truth of one or more other related statements, which are the premise or premises. An *"argumentative text,"* then, is just a writing (such as an essay or newspaper opinion piece) in which the author attempts to prove the truth of a conclusion based on the truth of one or more other statements, which are her premises.

What does it mean to be a "better reader"? It could mean any number of things. In a book teaching speed reading, for example, being a "better reader" likely would mean reading faster than you do now. For our purposes, a "*better reader*" is a reader who is able to better analyze, and hence, to better understand, the meaning of argumentative texts. (Notice that this paragraph itself gives you one of the tools to being a better reader—asking yourself what the author means when he uses ambiguous or broad terms, as is the term "better reader." We will use that tool in various ways throughout this book.)

The kinds of argumentative works we will use as examples are drawn from the mass media (opinion essays and editorials found in newspapers, essays on politics and current events, and the like), speeches, sermons, and academic disciplines (e.g., political science, psychology, philosophy), and books. In having a limited focus on argumentative texts, this book does not pretend to be a comprehensive introduction to the art of reading every type of text. There is plenty to learn within the limited subject matter selected here, and there are already many good books on how to be a better reader of works of fiction and poetry.

The tools we will discuss principally include concepts, techniques, methods, suggestions, tips, and skills that will allow you *to better analyze* argumentative texts. The focus here is on analytic tools because *analysis is essential to reading for understanding.* Better analysis leads to better understanding—deeper and richer understanding—of what you read. (Once you have mastered these tools, you will be better at constructing arguments and constructing more effective arguments, but that constructive task is not the principal focus of this book.) Along the way, we also consider some more general things to think about as you work to be a better reader.

The approach in this book is entirely practical and flexible—use the tools that work for you to make you a better reader. To be clear, "use the tools that work for you," does not mean that you should "follow your own instincts" in reading a text, or "accept any reading that *feels* good," or that "any reading is as good as any other reading."

Think of reading as an art, just like throwing a football, cooking a good meal, painting a watercolor, or making a piece of furniture are arts. There are better and worse ways to perform any artistic task—some quarterbacks have better judgment than their competitors, some cooks have a better sense of flavor—and there are tools and techniques commonly used by those who are better at their art than those who are less skilled.

So, "use the tools that work for you" means that there are tools and techniques you *can* and *should* master to have a deeper understanding of what you are reading, to be better at the art of reading. It also means that these tools will be best applied by different readers in different ways at different times in developing their reading skills. Depending on where you are in advancing your reading skills, you may find some parts of this book easy and other parts more challenging. That is to be expected. The important point is that by applying the tools in this book diligently you will rise to the challenges, become a better reader, and master the sections that are now obstacles for you.

One implication of this flexible approach is that you will not find in this book a set of rules to follow that will make you a better reader. Rules have their place. You cannot play football or drive a car in a city without them. Their place, however, is not in this book. One problem with any list of rules for reading argumentative texts is that their meaning and proper application are very context-specific.

This book could not possibly guide you through every text you will encounter and show you how a particular rule may, or may not, apply. Moreover, rules often conflict: "Never skim a text" vs. "Always begin a work by skimming the text"; "Never stop and reread a chapter until you are done reading the complete book" vs. "If you don't understand a chapter, go back and reread it before going on." Conflicting rules often lead to confusion. That will cause you to be frustrated, and that is not productive. Worst of all, studying the "10 Rules to Be a Better Reader" or "The Ten Commandments of Reading" is no fun. To paraphrase the former American Poet Laureate Ted Kooser, "part of the fun of practicing the art of reading comes from the freedom to choose."[3]

The approach in this book is practical and flexible in another sense. As you read this book you will note that the tools we discuss do not depend on any academic theories or jargon. We do not discuss psychological theories of how thinking is influenced by rationality, emotions, manipulation by the mass media, confirmation biases, or a host of other factors. There is no reliance here on academic theories of emotional intelligence, conventional intelligence, how we learn, the sociological influences on thinking, and many other topics that are of interest to social scientists and English professors. You can read. That means you can learn the tools presented in this book, even if you have absolutely no familiarity with theories of reading, learning, thinking, education, communications, or the technical terms that permeate the related academic disciplines.

MEANING

Our focus will be on the principal sources of the meaning of an argumentative text. "Meaning" is a broad and ambiguous term, as any good dictionary or book on the philosophy of language will demonstrate. For our purposes, "*meaning*" refers to the thoughts and emotions that the author intends to communicate to you, the reader. The principal sources of meaning we will discuss are:

1. *Structure.* The structure of a text gives it meaning, in much the same way that an animal's skeleton gives it shape and provides the framework to which the muscles are attached. We will consider the following questions:
   - Does the text have a beginning, middle, and end?
   - What do they say?
   - Do they hang together (have some sort of logical order), or not?
   - Is this sentence or paragraph really necessary to the point the author is trying to prove?
   - If not, why does the author include it? What meaning does it contribute to the text as a whole that otherwise would not be there if it were omitted?
   - If so, what does it add to proving her thesis?
   - What are the relations of the major points of the text to each other?
   - What is the relation of the evidence presented to this or that major point in the text?

Accordingly, we will examine various types of introductions (chapter 5) and discuss the importance of outlining and summaries (chapter 6).

2. *Key sentences, phrases, and words.* It is elementary that to understand what an author means you need to understand the key sentences, phrases, and words she uses.
   - Analyzing ambiguous sentences, phrases, and words (that is, sentences, phrases, and words that have more than one reasonable meaning) is essential to understanding many argumentative texts.
   - Because not all uses of language refer to facts and not all are to be taken literally, we also discuss statements that express norms and values (normative statements), statements that do not mean what they literally say but that may add color or nuance to a text (irony), and the use of rhetorical appeals to emotions, feelings, or shared values, or to the credibility or reputation of the writer, as a means of persuading the audience to act in some fashion or to have certain emotions.

We address these topics in chapter 7.

3. *Context.* Many argumentative texts are part of an ongoing debate on some issue in culture, politics, or a specific academic discipline. Understanding the context of a work in the flow of the ongoing debate of which it is a part often is essential to understanding what the author means, why she takes the time to make this point or that one, and what motivates her to write the piece at all. When you walk into a movie in the middle, you can understand the words the actors are speaking, but because you do not know the narrative context of those words, you are likely to miss many of their implications and nuances. It is no different with argumentative texts. When the author is not expressly participating in an ongoing dialogue on an issue, there generally is a more diffuse social, political, or cultural context that motivates the work and gives it meaning. The physical environment referred to in or implied by a text also may operate as a context to give the text meaning.

Context is the subject of chapter 8.

4. *Logical Connections Between Terms.* Every argument relies on logic in some fashion. So, to understand what an author means, it is useful to understand some basic rules of logic and types of logical mistakes. Some statements are blatantly illogical. Your Uncle Larry can *say*, "it's raining and it's not raining," but that would not tell you what he really thinks about the weather. Uncle Larry may also say, "today is Monday and today is Friday" and that would not tell you what day he believes it is. Most authors do not engage in these clear forms of illogical reasoning, but they make many other logical mistakes that obscure their meaning or that show that their conclusion is not supported by their premises.
- Knowing the most common mistakes, and some other basic rules of logic, are extremely useful tools for extracting the meaning from an argument, and for knowing when an argument fails to prove what it is attempting to prove.
- Similarly, knowing a fundamental logical distinction—between necessary and sufficient conditions—is extremely useful in understanding arguments and whether an author has stated her argument clearly and proven her conclusion.

So, we cover some introductory logic in chapter 9.

In addition to discussing these sources of meaning, we will analyze argumentative texts and do exactly the same sort of work you will do when you try to wrestle the meaning out of a text. For simple texts, with clear arguments, such wrestling will not be much of a challenge for you. For the most complex works, it could be the work of years (ask a professor in an English or philosophy department). Bear in mind that the difference between a "simple" text and a "complex" one is far from self-evident. In the first section of this chapter we saw that an eight-sentence text message about eating ice cream could be reasonably interpreted in several ways. Despite initial appearances, maybe it is not a "simple" text, or at least not as simple as you first thought.

The tools we discuss in this book are generic and apply across all argumentative texts and academic disciplines. The discussion of the particular styles of argumentation and the vocabulary of each of the many particular academic disciplines—and, accordingly, how your understanding of these styles and vocabulary will enhance your understanding of a text in any particular discipline—is beyond the scope of this book.

HOLD ON TO THIS THOUGHT

Before we begin discussing the many tools that will enable you to be a better reader, let's step back for a moment and look at the big picture. Consider two quotes. The first is from a speech Ralph Waldo Emerson gave in 1837:

> Books are the best of things, well used. . . . They are for nothing but to inspire.[4]

Emerson lived in the 19th century, in the small village of Concord, Massachusetts. He was white, a Unitarian minister, and a widely influential essayist, poet, and lecturer.

The second quote is from Malcolm X. When serving seven years in prison for burglary, Malcolm X effectively taught himself how to read. In reflecting on that experience he wrote:

> I have often reflected upon the new vistas that reading opened to me. I knew right there in prison that reading had changed forever the course of my life.[5]

Malcolm X was an African American, born in Omaha, Nebraska, in 1925, and grew up in large cities (Lansing, Michigan, and Boston, Massachusetts). In his younger years he was a small-time criminal, later became a follower of the Nation of Islam and, in the early and mid-1960s, was an influential civil rights leader.

These are two very different historical figures. In a sense, Emerson and Malcolm X come from different worlds. And yet, they both champion the benefits of reading. They independently affirm that reading inspires and can change your life in the most fundamental ways. Reflect on this, think about it, now and as we proceed.

NOTES

1. It may seem odd to call an argument "theoretical" when its conclusion is a fact or opinion that is not part of a scientific or mathematical theory. The reason for this is historical. For many centuries, philosophers have distinguished reasoning that attempts to prove something about the world—which they called "theoretical" or "speculative" reasoning—from reasoning that is action-guiding—which they called "practical" reasoning. Because that usage is well-established and you may encounter it elsewhere in your studies, we will follow it here.

2. This passage is based upon an opinion essay by John W. Fitzpatrick and Peter P. Marra, "The Crisis for Birds Is a Crisis for Us All," *New York Times,* September 19, 2019, available at https://www.nytimes.com/2019/09/19/opinion/crisis-birds-north-america.html.

3. Ted Kooser, *The Poetry Home Repair Manual*, p. 35 (Lincoln, NE: Univ. of Nebraska 2007). The original quote is, "Part of the joy of writing, or of practicing any art, comes from the freedom to choose."

4. Ralph Waldo Emerson, "The American Scholar" in *The Portable Emerson*, pp. 23, 29 (New York: Viking Press 1972).

5. Malcolm X, *The Autobiography of Malcolm X*, p. 182 (New York: Ballantine 1965).

Chapter 2

Reading Is Not a Spectator Sport

The reading of all good books is like a conversation with the noblest men of past centuries who were the authors of them.—Rene Descartes (French philosopher and mathematician, 1596–1650), *Discourse on the Method*, Part I (1637)

This book provides you with tools for improved understanding of argumentative texts and strategies and tips for how to use them. Why do you need such tools? Because, as we said in the prior chapter, reading is an art, like cooking, making furniture, or throwing a pass in football. Each art has tools that are suited to that art, that activity. The tools used in the art of cooking are suited to cooking and are no good on the football field or in painting a watercolor. So, before you learn the tools, it will be productive to examine briefly, what kind of art, what kind of activity, is reading.

WATCHING THE GAME VS. PLAYING THE GAME

In our visual culture, you may be under the illusion that reading is like watching a football game or a movie. You may think about reading along these lines: (1) football players play the game and I am a spectator passively watching them play, (2) similarly, the author has written the book and I passively soak up what she has written, (3) watching football requires not being distracted (especially if it is an important game), (4) reading requires not being distracted, so (5) reading is like watching football.

Does that sound right to you? Well, it is not. Reading is not a spectator sport. Reading is an activity, an activity like *playing* football or basketball, or like *making* a cake, or *engaging in* a deep conversation with a friend. It is not passive. It is the difference between watching your friends exercise at the gym and vigorously exercising yourself.

When you go to the pages of a book, an essay, or a serious article, if you want to exercise your mind, to make it more fit, to expand it, to pass a test or graduate from college, you need to use the equipment—your intellect, your experiences, and the words on the page—and you can only use these if you have eliminated the distractions and do some sustained heavy lifting. Reading is active, sustained mental exercise, just like lifting weights or riding a bicycle is active physical exercise. You set the goals and you do what needs to be done to achieve them.

What does it mean to say that reading is an activity *like* playing football, making a cake, acting in a movie, or lifting weights at the gym? It means, to start, that reading it is not *the same* as any of those other activities. One obvious difference is that reading is a mental activity and these other activities are physical.

But what kind of mental activity is reading? Reading for understanding, which is our focus here, is a form of communication. It is very close to having a deep conversation with a close friend. Think of it as a dialogue between the text and you. It is a dialogue in which you are continually *asking the next question* of the text to understand what the author means. The next question may be, for example: Why does he say that? or, what does he mean by that? or, has he proven that that point? This is fairly abstract. The following discussion will illustrate the point.

READING AS A DIALOGUE

Suppose your best friend took a position on an issue and you do not know why he holds that position. Maybe the issue is pro-life vs. pro-choice, or pro-death penalty vs. antideath penalty, or access to free, universal health care for all Americans, or the right of the U.S. government to spy on all of our emails and internet usage vs. rights to personal privacy.

Now there are two ways to respond when your friend asserts a position, say, about the death penalty. First, you can respond with words to this effect, "that's baloney" or "I agree." Or, second, you can say something like this, "let me understand where you are coming from (what you mean). Is it your view that the death penalty is justified for every unlawful act (even running a stop sign), or every violent crime with no exceptions, or every violent crime with some exceptions, or something else?"

If you proceed in the first way, whether you disagree ("that's baloney") or agree ("you're brilliant") with your friend's position, you are assuming: (1) that you understand your friend's position and (2) that you understand the reasons why he holds that opinion. If you make these assumptions when you disagree with your friend, the discussion then may well degenerate into each of you staking out your respective positions, followed by each of you trying to persuade the other that they are wrong. That often is not very productive. If you make these assumptions when you agree with your friend, then you can reaffirm the wisdom and truth of your shared view, congratulate yourselves that great minds think alike, and move on to another point of discussion, all the while never exploring whether you really understand and agree with the opinion your friend expressed. That is not intellectually very productive either.

What happens if you proceed in the second way, by trying to understand the particulars of your friend's view on the death penalty (what does he know, or claim to know?) and the reasons why he holds that opinion (how does he know it)? You begin to understand that view and whether it has a reasonable foundation of any sort and, if so, of what sort.

In a discussion on the death penalty, the dialogue between you and your friend may proceed along these lines.

> Friend: I'm in favor of the death penalty. I have no problem with executing people who break the law.
> You: Let me understand where you are coming from. Is it your view that the death penalty is justified for every unlawful act (like running a stop sign), or every violent crime with no exceptions, or every violent crime with some exceptions, or something else?
> Friend: I believe in the death penalty for any sort of violent crime that leads to physical injury or death to innocent people. (That is a start in clarifying his position and answering the "what does he know" question.)
> You: Why do you favor the death penalty in those circumstances? (You now are pressing the "how does he know it" question.)
> Friend: Because all of the sociological studies have shown that the death penalty deters crime. (He is relying on facts, data, to support his position.)
> You: Let's assume for a moment that you are right about all of those studies. If the death penalty deters crime and our society wants to deter crime, why aren't you in favor of the death penalty for serious crimes that don't involve physical injury to innocent parties, like bank robbery, extortion, burglary, cyberstalking, revenge porn, and the like?
> Friend: Because in those other crimes, the penalty is out of proportion to the crime.
> You: So, your position on the death penalty is not just based on the facts contained in all of those sociological studies, but it also is based on a moral principle that punishments should fit the crime?
> Friend: Yes.

You: Well, what about a case in which severe psychological harm is inflicted on a group of 50 people to the point of driving them insane or causing them severe mental illnesses, and there's no physical injury? For example, suppose they were held in solitary confinement for years and had to listen to extremely loud heavy metal music every day for 18 hours a day, and it drove them all crazy? Doesn't that sort of torture destroy a person even more than a minor gunshot wound from which they recover? And here, it's 50 people, not just one. Why doesn't the death penalty fit the crime in that case?

And with that question, your friend will need to further explain the basis for his position or modify it to include the type of case you described. His response will take the dialogue in one of many different possible directions. Since this is not a book about the death penalty, we need not discuss what that response may look like. Instead, let's pause and discuss this example.

Suppose your friend modifies his view to include cases of severe psychological injury of the sort you have described. His views are a moving target, a wrestling opponent who will not keep still. What does that teach us about reading argumentative texts?

Two possibilities suggest themselves. On one hand, it could mean that having a dialogue with a friend is different from reading a text. Unlike a conversation, the words in the text are fixed, and the author does not get to change his position when you, the reader, start asking tough questions. On the other hand, it could also suggest that the *process* of understanding the meaning of a text is not so far different from engaging in a serious dialogue with a friend.

We often start our process of understanding a text by thinking something like, "Okay, I get it. Her thesis is X and her reasons for it are A, B, and C." But in many cases, our understanding of the thesis and the reasons for it do not align very well, leaving us confused, or leaving us with the opinion that the author is confused or has not done a very good job of supporting her thesis. It is just at that point, when you press the analysis further, when you begin to dig deeper into a text, that you refine your understanding of what the author is trying to say and why she says it. And in that sense, the author's thesis does change from your perspective—you have a better understanding of what that thesis is and why she holds it. In that sense, analyzing a text is not so far different from your death penalty dialogue with a friend and his changing views in the course of that dialogue.

Reading for understanding can best be viewed as a dialogue between you and the text, or more precisely, between your current understanding of the text and what the author is trying to communicate, which in many cases will not be the same as your current understanding. Trying to uncover the author's meaning is not like digging for a buried treasure chest—where you either find the thing or you do not. When the argument is a difficult one, it is a lot more like a wrestling match where the opponent is moving and trying to evade getting pinned down.

So, how do you pin down an author's meaning? In a sense, this entire book attempts to answer that question. Let's start with an answer that may seem like a mundane cliché: you need to understand both the big picture and the details.

The Big Picture. What path did you take to get to this chapter, this page? Did you skip right by the table of contents, the preface, and begin your reading with chapter 1? Did you skip all of those *and* chapter 1, and begin your reading with this chapter? If you answered "yes" to either of these questions, why did you take that path?

For most argumentative books that you are going to read to understand, the most productive strategy usually is to *get the big picture first*. You do that by: reading the table of contents, preface, and introduction; looking closely at the chapter titles; and reading the back cover. If you are reading the type of book where authors usually take sides on an issue, say a political or religious issue, it may also be helpful to do a quick search online to learn your author's political or religious views and her institutional affiliations.

Why is the big picture important, especially when reading an argumentative book? Because the contents of any particular chapter have meaning in the context of the work as a whole. Context imparts meaning to a text. That context includes not only the topics covered in the other chapters in the book, but also the intellectual or other (religious, political, etc.) leanings or biases that the author brings to her work. Knowing the big picture, you will be far better prepared to extract the meaning of the text of each chapter, and specifically, you will be far better positioned to see how the ideas presented are related and how the parts of the author's argument are connected. We will discuss context further in chapter 8.

Try it now. If you have not done so already, go back and read the table of contents, the preface, and chapter 1 of this book, and the chapter headings and back cover, and then ask yourself whether you have a better idea of what we are trying to accomplish through this book.

If you jumped straight to this chapter as a way of cutting corners, *the first takeaway for you is this: now is not the time to cut corners in your reading of an argumentative text. Your second takeaway is: very rarely will there be a time to cut corners in your reading.* If you are absolutely forced to cut corners in your reading (which I do not recommend), do so only with full attentiveness to what you are doing and why you are doing it, so that you do not come away from the text with, at best, a rudimentary or seriously flawed understanding of what you are reading.

Who's Lurking in the Details? Did you ever hear the expressions "God is in the details" or "the Devil is in the details"? Leaving aside the theological debate as to which of these aphorisms may be right, both teach us that something really important is going on in the details of any argumentative text, and so *you need to pay attention to the details*. When you understand the details, and how they fit into the broader text, then very likely you have pinned down your moving opponent.

Consider how the attention to details applies in the hypothetical death penalty dialogue. How often have you thought (or heard someone say) that such-and-such a position is wrong because the other person just does not understand the facts? Undoubtedly, there are many times when that complaint is true. But in the death penalty dialogue, you are willing to accept the truth of all of the facts contained in the sociological studies your friend relies upon, and yet that still does not fully explain his position. You still do not fully understand his position even if you agree (for the sake of the argument) that he has his facts correct.

In addition to all of those facts, to understand his position you also need to know that it incorporates an ethical rule as well, namely, that a punishment should be proportional to, should "fit," the crime. And, before the discussion ends, you also need to fully understand how far he holds that principle and whether there are any other ethical rules or other nonfactual assumptions embedded in his view. Are there, for example, practical limits to how far he thinks the death penalty should be applied, given the many imperfections of our criminal justice system? In short, you *at least* need to know that he is resting his view on more than just agreed-upon facts and what those other nonfactual bases are.

Pressing an author's position to understand all of the foundations for that position—facts, ethical or moral views, opinions as to what is and is not practically achievable, views on human nature, assumptions about culture, and so on—is essential to understanding many argumentative texts. Indeed, if you do not understand what each of those bases are and how they play into an author's argument, it is quite possible that you do not have a good understanding of the text, you have not pinned down your moving opponent.

Beyond an attention to the salient details, notice that to engage in the death penalty dialogue with your friend requires that both of you have patience, persistence, openness, and intellectual honesty. These are essential to being a better reader than you are now. They are traits that can be developed with practice—no one is born with them. Just like being a better wrestler, chess player, or cook comes from practice.[1]

"Persistence" is a polite way of saying that you must be intellectually aggressive. The difference between being a poor reader, an average reader, and a good reader is often a function of how intellectually aggressive you are in wrestling the essential meaning from the text. Sometimes you need to grapple with a text like an aggressive wrestler grapples with an opponent to win the match. You pin down your author's meaning *by always asking the next question*: Why does the author say this? What sense is the author making when he says this? Why does he focus on this fact and ignore that one? Is he relying on a moral principle buried deep in his argument? Does this conclusion really follow from his premises or is his reasoning faulty? And so on. We will see many examples of "asking the next question" in the chapters that follow.

Let's pause for a moment and reflect on this chapter before we go on. Some of you who are reading this book may believe that reading is a lot of work and not much fun. If you fall into that category, here is some good news—the more you read, the more you will like it. Like so many other worthwhile things you do in life, practice enhances your skill and enjoyment of the activity.

Here is more good news: you can do it. You definitely can be better at reading than you are now. A lot of people like you have done it.

Here is still more good news. There is a payoff—and you get to decide what the payoff is. You get to pick why you want to be a better reader and what you want to get out of reading better. Do you want to pass a history course, get a better job, earn more money, graduate from school? Then read better, read smarter.

Here is the bottom line: being a better reader cannot hurt your chances to get what you want out of life and it certainly will improve them. No downside, just some mental exercise with no limits on the upside. That is a hard deal to pass up.

Reading is freedom. Reading is liberation. It will take you places you want to go. It will take you places you did not even know existed. And that journey will leave you enthralled and empowered. (Remember those quotes from Emerson and Malcolm X in chapter 1.)

NOTE

1. For one author's views on the virtues needed to be a good reader, see Damon Young, *The Art of Reading* (Melbourne: Scribe 2018).

Chapter 3

Why Are You Reading?

Reading is a basic tool in the living of a good life.—Joseph Addison (British magazine publisher, essayist, and politician, 1672–1719)

Whenever you are engaged in any activity, it is always a good idea to know why you are doing it. So, why are you reading?

Every activity has a purpose, an end, a goal. Your ultimate goal in reading any book, article, or essay may be to pass a course, to get a job, or to impress a girlfriend. Each of those goals may be important to you. And properly so. We are not going to address them here. Rather, we are concerned now with goals that are more closely tied to the activity of reading itself, whatever your other goals in life.

Here are three of the principal purposes of reading.

READING TO UNDERSTAND

The purpose of this book is to provide you with tools that enable you to better understand argumentative texts. So, we will begin our discussion of the purposes of reading by discussing what it means to read for understanding.

A wonderful teacher once said in a lecture that the principal aim of education is to teach us to ask two questions of any author: (1) what does he know? and (2) how does he know it?[1] When we ask, "what does an author know," think of that as equivalent to asking, "what is the author's conclusion (his thesis)?" When we ask, "how does he know it?" we are asking, "what are the premises that lead to that conclusion?" If you can answer both of those questions for any argumentative text, then you *understand the argument*. That sounds a lot simpler than it is. For most texts (other than the simplest ones), you will need to engage in analysis to figure out what the premises and conclusion of the argument are and what they mean (especially when their meaning is not clear). That involves interpreting particular sentences of the text that you think are parts of the argument and those that you think are not parts of the argument. The sentences that you think are not part of the argument may clarify or obscure the meaning of the argument, emphasize or de-emphasize certain parts of the argument, make the argument more or less persuasive, or be irrelevant to the argument. *Understanding the meaning of an argumentative text requires understanding the argument and, in addition, understanding the meaning of the parts of the text that are not part of the argument and their relation to the argument.* Why are those other parts there? What is the author trying to say by including them?

If this sounds a bit abstract, go back to chapter 1 and see how this point applies to our analysis of your friend's ice cream text. One of the important lessons of our discussion there is that "the argument" of a text does not refer to a series of statements that are etched in stone, that we can point to and say with absolute certainty, "this is the argument and nothing else in the text is part of the argument." Recall that in our analysis of the ice cream text, what we finally determine to be the premises of the ice cream argument depends, in part, on what meaning we think the author intends by the sentences "You'll feel like an April day, like springtime" and "The store's across the street from you." What we take to be "the argument" depends, in part, on how we interpret those sentences, what meaning we give to them. Because interpretation is an art, it can be performed with more or less skill. It leads to better and worse readings of argumentative texts, but not absolutely "right" and "wrong" readings.

At some point in your life—past or future—it is virtually certain that you have been or will be part of a discussion about what a passage in a text means. The text might be a passage in the Bible, a clause in the United States Constitution, or an editorial in the *New York Times*. These debates are inevitable and certain to continue. No matter how tightly an author attempts to frame an argument or write an argumentative text, it is just in the nature of our language that the text will be open to multiple interpretations (unless the argument is extremely simple, as in our many Socrates examples). Meaning is flexible and often not entirely transparent. On top of that, for most of the argumentative texts that you will read, especially those in the mass media, the authors have not gone to extraordinary lengths to write tight arguments. Accordingly, the possible interpretations of these texts multiply.

In brief, we live in a world of argumentative texts, for which, *within a zone of reasonableness, there is no test or rule by which it can be determined for all purposes that a reading of an argumentative text is authoritatively (beyond dispute) "right" or "wrong." There is no one authoritative reading of a text. We have only readings that are better (more careful, more nuanced, and more insightful) and worse (less careful, less nuanced, and less insightful).* (That's another tool for your reading toolbox.) In contrast, there is a single, right answer to many math problems (such as, what is the square root of 144? or, how many total degrees in the four angles of a square?).

To illustrate, suppose a Major League Baseball player strikes out every time he is at bat and he sets the league record every year for errors in the field. No one would really dispute seriously that the player is a "bad" player and should not be in the major leagues. But suppose two Major League Baseball players have a similar mix of offensive and defensive skills, those skills go up and down over the course of several years, and they are statistically average players. Both of them belong in the major leagues, but there is no single test to measure who is the better baseball player now or who will be better next year. Similarly, unless your reading of a text is clearly "bad," there is no test by which to judge whether your reading of a text, or another reading, is "right" or "wrong."

So, how do you know if your reading is "bad," outside the zone of reasonableness, like the "bad" baseball player who should not be in the majors, or whether it is at least a reasonable reading given what the text actually says? We can state a few characteristics that mark a reading as "bad," that are the equivalent of our terrible baseball player's strikeouts and errors, that define the zone of reasonableness for an interpretation of an argumentative text.

1. The reading is contradicted by or is contrary to what the author expressly states.
   - You say the author holds position X (e.g., the death penalty is always moral) when the author explicitly states that she holds not-X (e.g., the death penalty is never moral). You have contradicted the author. This may happen when an author is misquoted, but that is not the only way to contradict what the author has written.
   - You say the author holds position X (e.g., the death penalty is always immoral) but the author actually holds position Y (e.g., the death penalty is immoral only in certain circumstances), where the author cannot hold both X and Y, but Y does not directly contradict X. You have taken a position that is contrary to the author's position.
2. The reading cannot be inferred from (is not implied by) what the author expressly states.
   - Suppose your reading of a text is that the author holds position X even though the author never explicitly says X. That in itself is not a problem if what the author has written actually implies X. But your reading is not reasonable, is "bad," if you cannot take what the author expressly states and derive X from those words by any logical reasoning. You have simply attributed to the author views (likely, your own views) that she has not expressly or implicitly adopted in her text.

3. The reading is not directly contradictory to what the author expressly states, but is grossly incomplete. It does not acknowledge much of what the author has actually written.
   - In this case, the reading is not full and complete like a realistic painting or photograph of the author's meaning, but is like a stick figure or a cartoon rendering of the author's meaning.
4. The reading commits the author to a nonsensical or obviously factually false position. Virtually every author of an argumentative essay or book is sufficiently rational not to write nonsense (like "quadruplicity stardust mooga") and to know and acknowledge some unarguable facts ("the moon is not made of green cheese"). If your interpretation of a text commits the author to a position that is nonsensical or obviously factually false, that is a compelling sign that it is a "bad" reading.

When a reading does not have one or more of these flaws, then it at least deserves to be taken seriously; it very likely is within the zone of reasonableness; it is in the right ballpark playing the right game. When it yields new insights into a text or the problem the text is addressing, so much the better. Then we have strong evidence that the reading is on the better end of the spectrum.

So, how do you get into that zone of reasonableness, to a reading of a text that is not "bad" and may even be "good"? The point of reading for understanding is to attempt, as nearly as is possible, to understand the thoughts and emotions the author intends to communicate to the reader, what she means.

This means, *first*, not jumping immediately from reading to criticism and skipping understanding altogether. Professor Mark Edmundson teaches us:

> The art of interpretation is to me the art of arriving at a version of the work that the author . . . would approve and be gratified by. The idea is not perfectly to reproduce the intention; that can never be done. Rather, the object is to bring the past into the present and to do so in a way that will make the writer's ghost nod in something like approval. That means operating with the author's terms, thinking, insofar as it is possible, the writer's thoughts, reclaiming his world through his language.[2]

There is always a place for criticism. Its proper role is to be an aid to understanding or a result of understanding. It is not a goal to be achieved by skipping understanding altogether. *Understanding should precede any final critical judgment*—that is an essential tool for your reading toolbox.

Sometimes we read an article or essay and immediately form the opinion, "this is wrong . . ." or "she's absolutely right" before we really do any analysis. When you have such an immediate reaction, ask yourself, "do I really understand this piece, what the author means?" Your immediate reaction to a text (even if it is a favorable reaction) can be, and should be, the path that leads you to a better and more sophisticated reading of the text. So, if you find yourself immediately criticizing before really trying to understand the text, that is okay. Use that initial critical reaction as a door to lead you to better understanding, as an aid to understanding. Use your tools of analysis (the ones you are learning in this book) to test and refine your initial reaction. When you have completed the analysis, when you have an understanding of what the author means (as best as you can make it out), then return to your initial criticism (or favorable view) and ask yourself whether it needs to be refined, amended, or rejected in light of that analysis. Whatever your final critical judgment, it will be informed by and the result of your understanding of the text.

Reading for understanding means, *second*, not jumping immediately from reading to judging what you think the author is trying to communicate because you come to the work with preconceived ideas as to whether she is right or wrong about some subject, or because you have skipped over the tough part of the argument and instead have substituted your own (sometimes unreflective, unsupported, or otherwise half-baked) views as to what she must be saying in this or that chapter. *If you cannot answer the questions, "where in the text does she say that?" or "where does the actual text imply that?" by pointing to one or more passages that support your reading, then your reading may well have stepped outside the zone of reasonableness.* Use this tool for better understanding frequently.

Not all reading is reading for understanding, of course. So, if we are reading, but not reading for understanding, what are we doing? What is the goal? It is worth considering two other purposes of reading, contrast them with reading for understanding, and thereby sharpen this idea of reading an argumentative text to understand it.

READING TO OBTAIN INFORMATION

Sometimes we read only to get a particular piece of information. "Information" refers to facts and data. You may read a list of phone numbers to find the number of a distant relative, or read a recipe to find out how to bake chocolate chip cookies, or read a dictionary to learn how to spell a word, or read a weather report for a city you are going to visit, or read a Wikipedia blurb to find out which movie won the Oscar for best picture in 2018.

Facts and data by themselves are not arguments, although they can be used in formulating arguments. Think of how a list of the presidents of the United States differs from a biography of any one of those presidents. You can read this list to find out whether Lincoln was the fifteenth or sixteenth president of the United States. But to find out whether Lincoln was the greatest U.S. president ever or how good he was as commander in chief, you need a biography or history that makes an argument about Lincoln's conduct in those roles.

Note how differently you would read a list of presidents from how you would read the biography. In hunting for information, we tend to be very selective—if you only want to know whether Lincoln was the fourteenth, fifteenth, or sixteenth president, then you likely do not care about any other president (Washington or Franklin Roosevelt), and so you can skip the information about them. But in reading a biography, if you really want to learn about the subject of the work—what he did or did not accomplish, his successes and failures, his beliefs and motives—you generally need to read the entire book, to learn the things you wanted to know and a lot of other things you did not even know you did not know. And, if you want to understand *the author's argument* about the man or woman who is the subject of the biography, you have to read the entire work. Selectivity has little to no place here.

It is important to obtain and retain information. It is hard to see how any of us could do anything without it (if you do not know where the ice cream store is, you are unlikely to get there to buy an ice cream cone). But simply knowing facts, or knowing how to obtain information, is different from understanding an argument and the meaning of the text in which it is embedded.

READING TO BECOME WISE

Sometimes people read a book to feel the emotional life of the author, to see the world through the unique perspective of an author, to experience through the author's voice events and actions that are far removed from everyday life. People read, and reread, Shakespeare's plays, Thoreau's *Walden*, and Hemingway's *For Whom the Bell Tolls* for these reasons. Reading for these reasons does not have a standard, common name. Let's call it reading to become wise, for lack of a more serviceable label.

"Wisdom" is an old-fashioned word. It does not have much currency these days. It would be a fool's errand to pretend to give you an authoritative definition of it. This will have to do for now: wisdom is some largely unfathomable and rare combination of knowledge, perceptiveness, emotional sensitivity, and judgment acquired through many varied experiences. A wise man or woman is one who is better able to answer the "big questions" of life in some satisfactory way—who am I? how ought one to live? is happiness our ultimate goal? what do I owe to others?

Reading to become wise is not the same as reading an argumentative text to understand the meaning of that text. There are tools that enable you to pin down the meaning of an argumentative text. There are no tools that allow you to wrestle wisdom from a text. So, acquiring wisdom is not what this book is about. The good news is that using the tools in this book to improve your understanding of argumentative texts may well facilitate your taking a few more steps on the lifetime path to wisdom.

> *No university would ask any student to devour literature as I did when this new world opened to me, of being able to read and* understand.—Malcolm X, *Autobiography of Malcolm X,* pp. 176–77

NOTES

1. I believe the teacher was the great rhetorician and literary critic Wayne C. Booth, but I cannot find any reference confirming that he actually said or wrote it.
2. Mark Edmundson, *Why Read?* p. 53 (New York: Bloomsbury 2004).

Chapter 4

Arguments: A Closer Look

There are probably words addressed to our condition exactly, which, if we could really hear and understand, would be more salutary than the morning or the spring to our lives, and possibly put a new aspect on the face of things for us. How many a man has dated a new era in his life from the reading of a book?—Henry David Thoreau, "Reading," in *Walden*

In chapter 1 we briefly touched on what an argument is and how to analyze a text to determine what parts of it constitute the argument and which parts do not. There we defined "*argument*" as:

The form of reasoning that states a conclusion (or thesis) and attempts to show that it is true based on the truth of one or more other related statements, which are the premise or premises.

This definition of "argument" may be intuitive for you. If not, think of "argument" in this way:

When an author asserts an argument, she is saying this to her readers: "if these statements (the premises) are true, then this statement (the conclusion) is also true"; or, "if you know that the premises are true (and I am telling you that they are), then you know that the conclusion is true."

In this chapter we are going to discuss the most important implications of these definitions. We will discuss certain characteristics of arguments, four types of arguments, when an argument is "good" or "bad," and how an argumentative text differs from other kinds of nonfiction texts.

Chapter 4

TWO MYTHS ABOUT ARGUMENTS

There is widespread consensus as to what an argument is. Nonetheless, some critical thinking and writing texts characterize arguments in ways that are incorrect or misleading. It is useful to address two of these mischaracterizations so that we are not mislead or confused by them in our later discussions.

> Myth #1: The conclusion of an argument must be a statement of a subjective opinion.[1]

At some point in your studies you may read a discussion of arguments and see a statement like Myth #1. It is incorrect. You can safely ignore it. The idea behind it is that objective facts are verifiable and so not subject to proof through argument.

This myth reflects a misunderstanding of the purpose and types of arguments. While some arguments are designed to demonstrate the truth of a subjective opinion or a debatable point, many others are not. These other arguments are intended to demonstrate (1) the truth of an objective fact that the reader (or listener) has not yet accepted as true or (2) that a conclusion the reader does accept as true is proven by premises which he did not know demonstrated the truth of that conclusion.[2] We have already seen one simple, time-honored example of such an argument:

> All men are mortal.
> Socrates is a man.
> Therefore, Socrates is mortal.

There is nothing subjective about the conclusion. It simply is (was) an objective fact that Socrates is mortal. The confirmation of that conclusion by the fact of his death does not mean that an argument cannot be used to prove the point. Here is another simple example of an argument with an objective, factual conclusion:

> All of our scientific evidence shows that since the formation of our solar system billions of years ago, within every twenty-four-hour cycle, for each place on the earth (except near the poles), there has been one sunrise and one sunset. [Premise]
> Accordingly, there is a very high probability that as long as our solar system exists, there will be one sunrise and one sunset every day in the place we now call Denver. [Conclusion]

If anyone cares to debate the conclusion, they can dispute the scientific evidence referenced in the premise, dispute the statistics that lead to the conclusion as to the high probability of the future daily sunrises and sunsets in Denver, or go to Denver to try to disprove the conclusion through repeated observation. The fact that someone may try to debate this conclusion does not make it any less objective or not subject to proof by argument.

This conclusion is not subjective in the way that your love of hip-hop or my dislike of peas are subjective. And the fact that someone might try to debate this conclusion does not mean that this is not an argument. Someone (an eighth grader, perhaps) may accept the conclusion based on personal experience ("every day I've lived in Denver, the sun has risen and set, so I expect it to do the same for as long as I'm alive"), and not know that it is also confirmed by scientific evidence.

> Myth #2. The conclusion of an argument must be a statement that can be proven true or false because it asserts that some state of affairs is or is not real.[3]

Myth #2 is partially right and partially wrong. The idea that this myth tries to capture is that many types of sentences cannot be the conclusion of an argument because they just are not the types of things that can be proven true or false, by an argument or otherwise (e.g., by observation). (For clarification, "state of affairs" is just a fancy way of talking about the way things and events are situated in the world, e.g., it is raining now, my car is red, and so on.)

These three types of sentences cannot be proven true or false and so they do not express statements that can be conclusions of arguments: (1) a greeting ("Dude ...," "Hi, Mom ..."), (2) a question ("how many planets are there?"), and (3) an exclamation ("hallelujah," "what the hell!").[4] To that extent Myth #2 is correct.

What about a command, an imperative, such as "Go eat ice cream!" or "No Parking"? As grammatical forms, these sentences do not express that some state of affairs is real or not; they cannot be proven true or false. In that respect, they would appear to be no different from greetings, questions, and exclamations, and so you might be tempted to conclude that they could not be conclusions to arguments. But that is not quite right. To see where it is wrong, let's go back to our discussion of the ice cream text in chapter 1.

Recall that the conclusion of the ice cream argument was "eat some ice cream." That is a command, an imperative. Your friend is commanding you to do something. As such, it cannot be proven true or false. And yet, we saw that it was the conclusion of a practical argument designed to show that someone—you—should or ought to do something. So, that conclusion could be restated as "you should (or ought to) eat some ice cream." We could also take common commands like "No Parking" and restate them as statements as to what someone "should" or "ought" not do. "You should not park here if you want to avoid a fine." Or, "you are concerned about public safety, so you ought not to park here."

These types of "should" and "ought" statements cannot be proven true or false by direct or indirect observation as can statements about some state of affairs in the world, such as, "the earth orbits the sun." Nonetheless, these terms (and others like them, such as "must") refer to a constraint on action, or a practical compulsion, imposed by some objective circumstances and the values or desires of the person or entity to whom they are addressed. Those constraints can be proven to exist or not through a practical argument. When they do exist, a statement that says that they exist is true, and when they do not exist, a statement that says that they do is false.

To make this fairly abstract point more concrete, the first three premises in this argument are the objective circumstances (a state of affairs) and the fourth premise expresses the addressee's wants or desires.

> On a hot, humid day, a person who eats ice cream will cool off. [Premise]
> It's a hot, humid day. [Premise]
> You don't have access to any means of cooling off other than eating ice cream. [Premise]
> You want to cool off. [Premise]
> Therefore, you should (ought to) eat some ice cream. [Conclusion]

The premises of this argument lead to the conclusion that a practical constraint exists on the addressee's future action. Such constraints are no less real, and no less capable of proof, than statements about the color of my car or the earth's orbit.

If Myth #2 is right, then (a) there would be no practical arguments or (b) any practical argument that concluded with an imperative sentence form, rather than its "should" or "ought" restatement, would by virtue of that mere grammatical form alone be deemed to be not an argument. Yet practical arguments have been recognized as legitimate arguments for more than 2,000 years (at least since Aristotle). Most importantly for present purposes, a great many of the arguments you will encounter in the mass media are practical arguments. These arguments encourage the government, corporations, unions, charities, or individuals to take some action—institute background checks on gun purchases, make health insurance available for all, lower taxes, drill for oil in Alaska, feed starving children, do not use plastic bags, and so on.

So, once we keep in mind the distinction between practical and theoretical arguments, we see that Myth #2 is misleading at best. It is true only if it is limited to theoretical arguments.

Note that my argument against Myth #2 is grounded in the premise that imperatives can be rephrased as "should" or "ought" statements, and vice versa. Because this book is about analyzing texts for their meaning, it is worth pausing for a moment and asking what meaning is gained or lost when we engage in such rephrasing. If you were to write an opinion piece for a blog, and the conclusion of your argument was, "Accordingly, the United States government should invest money in researching how to prevent a massive asteroid collision with the earth," no one would be confused by your meaning or think that conclusion out of place. Yet if you stated your conclusion in the blog post as an imperative, "Invest money in researching how to prevent a massive asteroid collision with the earth," it may well be received by your readers as odd. You, as a private citizen, have no power to issue commands to the federal government, and you may look foolish to write as if you do. On the other hand, if you were giving a speech to a rally of citizens concerned about asteroids colliding with the earth, your declarative conclusion, "Accordingly, the United States government should invest money (millions of dollars) in researching how to prevent a massive asteroid collision with the earth," may appear weak or technocratic. Your ringing imperative, however—"(And so to our government in Washington, I say,) invest money in researching how to prevent a massive asteroid collision!"—expressed with great emotion to a like-minded audience, may be entirely appropriate and viewed as a rousing call to action.

In brief, *the context in which an argument is made, and the way the argument is expressed, can be important in assessing its meaning.* For many or most practical arguments, rephrasing an imperative into a "should" or "ought" statement, and vice versa, should not result in any change of meaning, or if it does, it will be readily apparent and not problematic. We will consider normative statements ("should" and "ought" statements) in chapter 7 and will consider context further in chapter 8.

DEDUCTIVE AND INDUCTIVE ARGUMENTS

In chapter 1 we discussed two types of arguments—practical and theoretical. In this section we are doing to discuss another way to classify arguments—deductive or inductive. There is no one definition for a "deductive" or "inductive" argument, but a few general statements that are widely accepted will illustrate the differences between these two types.

A *deductive* argument is one in which the conclusion is said to follow *necessarily* from its premises, *whatever else may be true in the world.* Our argument proving that Socrates is mortal is an example of a deductive argument.

Whatever else is true in the world, if these premises are true—

All men are mortal and
Socrates is a man

then it *necessarily* follows that—

Socrates is mortal.

Here is an example of a deductive argument that is also a practical argument (because it tells someone to do something):

The only way to pass this course is to read the course book and study hard.
I want to pass this course.
Therefore, I must (should) read the course book and study hard.

You can easily find many discussions of deductive reasoning that state that deductive reasoning always proceeds from one or more general statements to a particular conclusion. This is incorrect. Some deductive arguments do this, as in our Socrates example. But not all. Here is a deductive argument that contains all general statements, including a general conclusion:

All rottweilers are mammals. [Conclusion]
We know this because:
All dogs are mammals, and.
All rottweilers are dogs.

(The order of the premises and conclusion is only a matter of style. It does not determine whether the text is attempting to state an argument or the type of argument.) Similarly, this deductive argument contains all general statements.

No dog is an insect.
All rottweilers are dogs.
So we conclude that no rottweiler is an insect.

A surprising number of arguments that you will read in the mass media are deductive arguments. They effectively state that the conclusion follows *necessarily* from the premises. Keep an eye out for them as we discuss arguments from the mass media in later chapters.

An *inductive* argument, by contrast, is one in which the conclusion is said to follow from the premises, not with necessity, but only *probably*, and with the implication that *other facts in the world could require that the conclusion be modified or abandoned*. Inductive arguments usually are grounded in data, evidence, or facts, and more or different data, evidence, or facts could change the conclusion. For example:

Rover is a brown dog and bites people.
Gus is a brown dog and bites people.
Jackson is a brown dog and bites people.
So, all brown dogs probably bite people.

If you have a larger data set—for example, if you studied 20 more brown dogs and none of them has ever bitten any person—your argument would look something like this:

Rover is a brown dog and bites people.
Gus is a brown dog and bites people.
Jackson is a brown dog and bites people.
Atom is a brown dog and has never bitten any person.
Bozo is a brown dog and has never bitten any person.
We know of 18 other brown dogs who have never bitten any person.
So, based on our available data, a small percentage of brown dogs bite people and a far larger percentage of brown dogs do not.

Sometimes inductive arguments are not obvious, as in these three examples.

The temperature in Dubuque has been over 90 degrees every 4th of July for the last 50 years.
So, the temperature in Dubuque on the next 4th of July probably will be over 90 degrees.

As in the Dubuque example, this inductive argument also relies on a discrete set of data:

Chuck: I've received 20 voice mails from politician X and every one of them contains only negative attacks on her opponent. I can only conclude that politician X has nothing positive to offer the voters.

Arguments by analogy[5] are inductive arguments:

As the general prosperity of a society increases, the physical health of its members improves.
Accordingly, it is likely that the increase in prosperity also improves the mental health of its members.

You can readily find discussions that state that inductive arguments always proceed from particular statements in the premises to general conclusions. This is incorrect. Some inductive arguments do that, as in our dog example, in which we generalize from Rover, Gus, and Jackson biting people to the conclusion that all brown dogs probably bite people. Some do not. Our example of the temperature in Dubuque on the 4th of July reasons from particulars (50 particular days) to a particular conclusion (the temperature on the next 4th of July).

Here is another example of an inductive argument that does not reason from particular premises to a general conclusion, but rather from many particular statements to another particular statement:

Dave says his electric vehicle always starts in cold weather.
Kathy says her electric vehicle always starts in cold weather.
Nick says his electric vehicle always starts in cold weather.
So, Judy's electric vehicle probably always starts in cold weather.

Similarly, the reasoning in this inductive argument is from all general premises to a general conclusion:

All ducks are waterfowl and have webbed feet.
All geese are waterfowl and have webbed feet.
All loons are waterfowl and have webbed feet.
Therefore, it is likely that all waterfowl have webbed feet.

It would be exceedingly rare to find an author expressly stating, "Dear reader, I'm making an inductive (or deductive) argument." But knowing the difference between them is extremely helpful in understanding the types of reasoning authors engage in when trying to prove a thesis.

Does the author fail to prove her conclusion simply because she has not looked at enough data or made a hasty inference based on the wrong sorts of data? That is an error in inductive reasoning that may be overcome by more data or a different sort of data.

Did the author fail to prove her conclusion because the argument is designed to establish the conclusion with necessity based only on premises stated, but that conclusion does not necessarily follow from those premises? That is a mistake in deductive reasoning and no amount of additional data or evidence can cure the logical error. There may be a way of proving the conclusion through different premises, but that would be to make a different argument. We will discuss such mistakes in reasoning in the next section and also in chapter 9.

So, we have used four terms to classify arguments—practical, theoretical, deductive, and inductive. How are these four types of arguments related?

These four ways of thinking about arguments are not mutually exclusive. A practical argument can be deductive or inductive. A theoretical argument can be deductive or inductive. A deductive argument can be practical or theoretical. An inductive argument can be practical or theoretical. All that may sound more confusing than it is. Table 4.1 clarifies the relations of these four types of arguments.

In short, there are four kinds of arguments: (1) deductive-practical, (2) deductive-theoretical, (3) inductive-practical, and (4) inductive-theoretical. We will discuss many examples of these in later chapters.

ARGUMENTS: VALID AND INVALID, STRONG AND WEAK

Not every argument that purports to prove a conclusion actually does that successfully. You know that already. At some point, you may have said to a friend, "bad argument, man" or, "hey, if you want me to do *that* you better come up with better reasons than *those*." In this section, we will discuss what it means for an argument to be "good" or "bad."

Deductive Arguments: Valid or Invalid

As we know, a deductive argument effectively says, *if* the premises are true (and I am telling you that they are), then the conclusion must be true, necessarily true no matter what else is true in the world. In logic texts, a deductive argument that is "good" because the conclusion necessarily follows from the premises is called a *valid* argument. A deductive argument is "bad" or invalid if the truth of its premises does not establish the truth of the conclusion. In an

Table 4.1. Four Types of Arguments

	Practical	*Theoretical*
Deductive	Deductive-practical	Deductive-theoretical
Inductive	Inductive-practical	Inductive-theoretical

invalid argument, *if* the premises are true, that does *not* necessarily establish the truth of the conclusion. Some of the deductive arguments we will examine in this book, and some of the deductive arguments you will encounter in your reading of argumentative texts, are valid and some are invalid. So, it is worth a few words to get this distinction clear.

To emphasize, a *valid* deductive argument is one in which, *if* the premises are true, the conclusion *necessarily* follows from them, no matter what else is true or false in the world. We see that with our Socrates example.

All men are mortal.
Socrates is a man.
Therefore, Socrates is mortal.

If the premises are true, there is no way for the conclusion to be false.

Consider this variation on our deductive Socrates argument:

Socrates is a man.
All men are bald.
Therefore, Socrates is bald.

Valid or invalid argument? It is valid. *If* all of the premises are true, then the conclusion must necessarily follow, no matter what else is true or false in the world. The second premise is false, of course, but *if* it were true, then there is no way the conclusion can be false.

Consider a second variation on our Socrates deductive argument:

All men are mortal.
Socrates is a man.
Therefore, Socrates is bald.

Valid or invalid? Even if the premises are true (as they are), the conclusion does not necessarily follow. Nothing stated in the premises makes it necessarily true that Socrates is bald. Even if as a matter of historical fact Socrates was bald, it is an invalid argument.

In addition to illustrating the distinction between a valid and invalid argument, these examples also emphasize that the validity or invalidity of a deductive argument is distinct from the truth or falsity of the sentences of which it is comprised. *Sentences are true or false*. Truth is a difficult philosophical topic. A lot of books and articles have been written about it. For our purposes, and to oversimplify matters, a sentence is true if and only if what it says corresponds to facts in the world. If I say, "a wombat is sleeping in my bed," that sentence is true if a wombat is actually sleeping in my bed, and it is false if a wombat is not sleeping in my bed. If you say, "the moon is made of recycled plastic," that sentence is true if the moon is actually made of recycled plastic and false if the moon is made of something else. A *deductive argument is not true or false* because, as a whole, it does not refer to anything in the world, even though the sentences of which it is comprised do.

This is an invalid argument even though all of its constituent sentences are true:

All men are mortal.
Socrates is a man.
So, we conclude that Socrates was a Greek philosopher.

It is invalid because the truth of the premises does not prove that the conclusion must be true.

This is a valid argument even though all of its sentences are false:

All dogs have six legs.
All cats are dogs.
Therefore, all cats have six legs.

It is valid because *if* the premises were true, then the conclusion necessarily would be true, whatever else is true in the world.

Here is one final example of an invalid deductive argument:

Rover is a large brown dog.
Large brown dogs always bite strangers.
Therefore, Rover is a German Shepherd.

Why is this argument invalid? Because even if the premises are true, it does not necessarily follow that the conclusion is true. Nothing stated in the premises proves that Rover is a German Shepherd rather than a poodle, a rottweiler, or a pit bull. The two premises can be true, but the conclusion could be true or false. In that case, the conclusion does not necessarily follow from the premises and the argument is invalid.

In reading for understanding, the distinction between valid and invalid deductive arguments is important. Except in cases of satire, parody, or deliberate attempts to deceive, no author intentionally propounds an invalid deductive argument. So, if you determine that an author's argument is invalid, you know his thinking is muddled or confused in some respect and that the meaning of his text will be similarly muddled or confused.

Inductive Arguments: Strong or Weak

In an inductive argument, the conclusion only follows from the premises with probability or a likelihood, not with necessity as in a deductive argument. To capture this difference, logicians do not use the terms "valid" and "invalid" to refer to "good" or "bad" inductive arguments. Rather, a "good" inductive argument is generally called a "strong" argument. Its conclusion follows from its premises with a higher likelihood or greater probability. A "bad" inductive argument is generally called a "weak" argument. Its conclusion only follows from its premises with a low probability.

Let's go back to a few of our examples at the beginning of this section and ask whether they are strong or weak inductive arguments. Recall this example:

> Rover is a brown dog and bites people.
> Gus is a brown dog and bites people.
> Jackson is a brown dog and bites people.
> So, all brown dogs probably bite people.

This is a weak inductive argument. A sample of three brown dogs out of all of the brown dogs in the world does not support the conclusion that all brown dogs probably bite people.

With a larger data set of 23 brown dogs, where some of them bite and some do not, and with a conclusion that is expressly limited only to the data referred to in the premises, the argument is strong.

> Rover is a brown dog and bites people.
> Gus is a brown dog and bites people.
> Jackson is a brown dog and bites people.
> Atom is a brown dog and has never bitten any person.
> Bozo is a brown dog and has never bitten any person.
> We know of 18 other brown dogs who have never bitten any person.
> So, based on our available data, a small percentage of brown dogs bite people and a far larger percentage of brown dogs do not.

Recall this example:

> Chuck: I've received 20 voice mails from politician X and every one of them contains only negative attacks on her opponent. I can only conclude that politician X has nothing positive to offer the voters.

This is a strong inductive argument because Chuck is basing his conclusion on a relatively large data set with uniform, consistent data.

Importantly, the strength or weakness of an inductive argument often has nothing to do with the size or uniformity of a given set of data. Consider this argument. Strong or weak?

> Every time Stanley goes fishing on a sunny day, he doesn't catch any fish. So, if you want to catch fish with Stanley, it's unlikely that you'll do it on a sunny day.

The argument attempts to draw a causal connection between the sunny skies and Stanley's poor fishing results; it says that the sunny days probably cause Stanley not to catch any fish.

The argument is weak, because it does not address any of the other causes that may affect Stanley's poor fishing results. Perhaps Stanley also does not catch any fish on any day that he goes fishing, whether it is sunny, cloudy, raining, or otherwise. Or, maybe he only goes fishing in a lake with no fish in it. Or, he may only fish on the very cold sunny days, when the fish are not biting. Or, he may be fishing in the wrong spots or using the wrong lures. And so on. The argument would be stronger if additional facts were introduced to establish the connection between the sunny weather and his not catching fish. What if the argument also contained these facts:

> Stanley catches a ton of fish every time he goes fishing on a cloudy, overcast day. But whether it's warm or cold, whatever lake he is fishing in, whatever lure he uses, he catches no fish when the skies are clear.

These additional premises would make the argument considerably stronger because by tending to exclude other factors that may cause Stanley to have bad results when he is fishing on sunny days, they make the connection stronger between sunny days and Stanley's poor fishing results.

Finally, recall this example from above:

> As the general prosperity of a society increases, the physical health of its members improves.
> Accordingly, it's likely that the increase in prosperity also improves the mental health of its members.

This is an inductive argument by analogy. It is in effect saying that whatever the connection is between increasing prosperity and improving physical health, that connection also holds between prosperity and mental health, because mental health is like physical health. Is it a strong or weak argument?

It is weak. A lot more information would be needed to establish that mental health and physical health are alike such that both show the same beneficial effects from increasing prosperity. For example, suppose a more prosperous society is one in which more people live in large urban environments, with lots of noise and crime, increased stress in their jobs, under systems of health insurance that cover physical illnesses but not mental illnesses, and so on. Then the connection between increasing prosperity and increasing mental health would be weak, even if physical health would be improving.

The distinctions between valid and invalid deductive arguments and strong and weak inductive arguments are important in reading for understanding. We will refer to them at various points in our discussions of argumentative texts in later chapters.

ENTHYMATIC ARGUMENTS: MEANING WHAT HE DID NOT WRITE

Most of the time when we are reading an argumentative text, we are trying to understand the meaning of what the author wrote. Often enough, however, we can figure out the meaning of what the author actually wrote only by assuming that he meant something that he did not write. In those cases, your task in trying to make sense of the text is to figure out what the author did not write but must have meant. It may sound bizarre. It is not. You are very familiar with it.

An argument in which the author has left one or more premises unstated is called an *enthymeme* or *an enthymatic argument*. Enthymemes are common in all sorts of argumentative texts. Suppose you are reading an argumentative text in which the author makes this (practical) argument:

Do you want to be healthier?
Eat more fiber.

This argument is enthymatic because it assumes that you, the reader, are not eating enough fiber to be as healthy as possible. It could be stated more fully and formally as:

You want to be healthier. [Premise]
You are not eating sufficient fiber to be as healthy as you can be. [Implied premise]
Eating more fiber than you are currently eating will cause you to be healthier. [Implied premise]
So, eat more fiber (or, you ought to eat more fiber). [Conclusion]

The author's imperative statement—"eat more fiber"—is telling you that the argument applies to you. Yet it applies to you only if the two additional premises are implied by what the author actually states. If you already are eating enough fiber to make you as healthy as possible, then the argument would not apply to you.

Consider this enthymeme:

Fifteen convicted murderers were executed last year in the United States.
I conclude that these executions were a grave injustice.

We know that this is an enthymatic argument because the conclusion does not follow from the premise alone. The conclusion does follow from the premise, however, if we add an implied premise. What would it be? Two possibilities immediately suggest themselves:

Fifteen convicted murderers were executed last year in the United States.
Capital punishment is always unjust. [Implied premise]
[Therefore,] these executions were a grave injustice.

Or,

Fifteen convicted murderers were executed last year in the United States.
The convictions in these cases were a violation of due process, based on no credible evidence, and should have been reversed on appeal. [Implied premise]
[Therefore,] these executions were a grave injustice.

The fact that there are two possible implied premises means that the argument is not clear and unambiguous.

There is no hard-and-fast rule that allows you to determine whether an argument is an enthymeme or is just so poorly drafted that it is impossible to imply a suitable missing premise. Your only option is to try to reconstruct the argument with possible candidates for an implied premise. If you cannot find a suitable candidate, then you likely are facing a poorly drafted argument or, perhaps, not an argument at all.

ARGUMENTATIVE TEXTS AND OTHER NONFICTION TEXTS

The discussion in chapter 1 and this chapter assumes that you are able to spot when a text is making an argument and when it is not. If only life were so simple. Reality is more complicated, and so it sometimes confounds the assumption. Accordingly, it is useful to spend some time generally clarifying how nonfiction argumentative texts differ from other kinds of nonfiction texts. Specifically, nonfiction argumentative texts are different from these types of nonfiction texts:

- expository
- descriptive
- explanatory
- rhetorical

Let's take a look each of these types more closely.

Expository Writing

An expository text, or an exposée (pronounced, ex-po-zay), is a writing that uncovers, reveals, or exposes some set of facts, events, theory, subject matter, or an interpretation of a text or work of art. You have seen exposées and read expository writing. You may have seen on television or read online or in a newspaper an expose of government corruption in your hometown, or of cost overruns on fighter planes purchased by the Defense Department, or of poverty in Kentucky. Textbooks that present a theory (such as Darwin's theory of evolution or Einstein's theory of general relativity) or a subject matter (on geometry, algebra, biology) are generally expository. A book of the rules of a game or of parliamentary procedure are expository.

Here is a sample paragraph from an expository writing that you might read in a newspaper:

> After an extensive investigation, our newspaper has uncovered substantial evidence of corruption in the Mayor's office in Emerald City. Our review of thousands of documents and interviews of numerous city employees reveals that the mayor's chief of staff has been taking kickbacks from contractors on road projects and from real estate developers. While we have not yet been able to determine precisely the amount of the kickbacks, we estimate them to be approximately $250,000. We have reason to believe that a grand jury is investigating these allegations of corruption, but have not been able to confirm this as of this edition of the paper.

The point of this paragraph is to expose, to uncover, facts that are otherwise not known to the readers. There is no argument here. The newspaper is not trying to prove that there is corruption by the chief of staff based on one or more premises. The article is simply showing *that* the newspaper knows there is corruption and how it came to know it.

If you want to learn how to play a game, or are in a dispute over the rules of a game, you might turn to *Hoyle's Rules of Games* to learn the established rules. Among the many games whose rules *Hoyle's* presents is the children's card game Old Maid:

> From a regular pack discard one queen. Deal the remaining cards out, one at a time, until all are dealt—they do not have to come out even. Two to eight may play. Each player discards, face up, all of his pairs (never three of a kind). Then each player in turn shuffles his hand and offers it face down to his left-hand neighbor, who draws one card, . . . [and so on].[6]

Again, there is no reasoning here from premises to conclusion. *Hoyle's* is simply stating, in effect, "if you want to know the rules of Old Maid, we are presenting them to you (here they are)."

Finally, here is part of the introduction to a book about Einstein's theory of general relativity.

> Einstein's general theory of relativity is a theory of gravitation which . . . also touches on the structure of space and time. It is easily the most widely accepted theory of gravitation available today; its study is an active and growing branch of modern theoretical physics. It is our purpose to understand what this theory is—how it works, what it has to say, what the physical phenomena are with which it deals, and what its predictions and applications are.[7]

If you want an argument about whether this theory is right or wrong, you will not find it here. If you want an exposition of the theory, this paragraph tells you that you have come to the right place.

Descriptive Writing

Nonfiction descriptive writing attempts to state the characteristics or traits of a person, place, thing, event, feeling, or state of mind. Here is an example:

> The moon rose over the desert, slowly. It was twice its normal size. Orangish-yellow in color. There I was, 18 years old, and I had never seen a moon so large and with such a color. For the first time in my life, I was in a state of awe. It was unexpected, a total surprise. The heat was rising from the desert floor, and I felt a slight wind began to blow.

Again, there is no argument here, no attempt to prove that X is true because premises Y and Z are true. It simply states the characteristics of a natural event (the moonrise) and the writer's mental and emotional reaction to it, and some other events (the slight wind) that the writer experienced. You could easily find this sort of writing in a work of nonfiction such as a travel guide or a book on the author's love of the desert.

Explanatory Writing

Suppose we were to read a slightly different version of the descriptive paragraph above about the moon rising over the desert. In this modified version, the paragraph states a cause of the large size and unusual color of the moon. It might go like this.

> The moon rose over the desert, slowly. It was twice its normal size. Orangish-yellow in color. I learned later that its unusually large size and unusual color were the result of the heat rising from the desert floor into the air, creating an optical illusion. There I was, 18 years old, and I had never seen a moon so large and with such a color. For the first time in my life, I was in a state of awe. It was unexpected, a total surprise. I felt a slight wind began to blow.

The fourth sentence provides an explanation of the cause of the unusual size and color of the moon. The author observed what was for him an unusual natural phenomenon and the fourth sentence tells us why that phenomenon occurred. There is no argument here, no attempt to prove that we can reason from premises X and Y to the truth of a conclusion, Z. There is no attempt to *prove* the causal relationship asserted in this paragraph. Instead, the author is simply telling us *what that relationship is* based on what he later learned.

Consider this brief causal explanation.

> For years scientists puzzled over the cause of the extinction of the dinosaurs. Our best scientific evidence tells us that around 65 million years ago a massive asteroid hit the earth, sent millions of tons of ash, smoke, and debris into the atmosphere, blocked out most of the sun's rays, and caused the mass extinction of all of the dinosaurs and 90% of all other life-forms.

This paragraph explains the cause of the mass extinction of the dinosaurs 65 million years ago. It does not present an argument because it does not ask the reader to reason from premises to a conclusion *that* the dinosaurs suffered a mass extinction or *that* the asteroid impact was the cause. Rather, it assumes that the extinction happened, and tries to explain *why* it happened.

Most of the explanatory writings you will encounter deal with causal explanations. Not all causal explanations, however, explain why one event, the effect (the eight ball went into the corner pocket), occurred by pointing to another event as its cause (because it was hit by the cue ball). For example, an explanation of why the planets orbit the sun may point to a force—gravity—and the masses of the planets and sun as the cause. Gravity (a force) and the masses of heavenly bodies are not events. So the explanation is causal, but it does not explain the happening of one set of events—planetary orbits—as the result of the happening of other events. Again, we might explain why the hospital was the only building in the city not to collapse during the earthquake by stating, "because it was made of flexible wood and not rigid concrete." That is a causal explanation of the hospital's survival but not one in terms of a causal event.

Rhetorical Writing

"Rhetoric" tends to have a bad reputation these days. Quite often the term is used to mean empty, uninformative speech, as in, "that's just a lot of empty political rhetoric and doesn't get to the problem." Or it is used to refer to speech that has an utter disregard for the truth and connotes an attempt to drown the reader or listener in falsehoods or irrelevant facts, as in "you're attempting to bamboozle me through a lot of false rhetoric." That is not the sense of rhetoric we are concerned with in this book.

Aristotle used "rhetoric" to refer to the use of words *to persuade* the reader or listener to act in some fashion, to believe something, or to feel something, either through (1) appeals to reasons and logical arguments, (2) appeals to emotions, feelings, or shared values, or (3) appeals to the credibility or reputation of the writer or speaker. An author would be using the term in this sense when she says, "Lincoln used soaring rhetoric in his second inaugural address." The use of rhetoric in this sense is especially common in argumentative texts written for a mass audience. Being able to recognize rhetorical statements, questions, and passages is an especially useful analytic tool to aid your understanding of the meaning of such texts.

We briefly touched on the concept of rhetoric in our ice cream example from chapter 1. Because you can never get enough ice cream, here it is again in full:

> Dude, it's summer. It's hot and humid—news flash. You want to cool off. Eat some ice cream. You'll feel like an April day, like springtime. The store's across the street from you. They have Cosmic Mix, your favorite flavor. If you want to try something new, go for Cherry Berry, my favorite.

You will recall that we discussed that your friend may have intended the last four sentences to be rhetorical. They may be appeals to your love of cool April days and springtime, your characteristic physical inertia ("crossing the street is no big deal"), your taste for Cosmic Mix and a willingness to try something new. On their face, the last four sentences do not state an argument. You cannot restate them into premises from which you can reason to a conclusion. Note also that your friend may have intended the first sentence and the second part of the second sentence ("—news flash") to be rhetorical. Your friend may have intended them to be slightly insulting—"Message received from Captain Obvious"—and with that appeal to your pride, to add greater force to the imperative, "Eat some ice cream."

President John F. Kennedy's inaugural address is generally regarded as one of the best inaugural addresses because of its grand rhetoric. Here are the initial paragraphs of that speech.

> We observe today not a victory of party but a celebration of freedom—symbolizing an end as well as a beginning—signifying renewal as well as change. For I have sworn before you and Almighty God the same solemn oath our forebears prescribed nearly a century and three quarters ago.
>
> The world is very different now. For man holds in his mortal hands the power to abolish all forms of human poverty and all forms of human life. And yet the same revolutionary beliefs for which our forebears fought are still at issue around the globe—the belief that the rights of man come not from the generosity of the state but from the hand of God.
>
> We dare not forget today that we are the heirs of that first revolution. Let the word go forth from this time and place, to friend and foe alike, that the torch has been passed to a new generation of Americans—born in this century, tempered by war, disciplined by a hard and bitter peace, proud of our ancient heritage—and unwilling to witness or permit the slow undoing of those human rights to which this nation has always been committed, and to which we are committed today at home and around the world.
>
> Let every nation know, whether it wishes us well or ill, that we shall pay any price, bear any burden, meet any hardship, support any friend, oppose any foe to assure the survival and the success of liberty.
>
> This much we pledge—and more.[8]

And then the speech continues with a series of pledges.

You can detect several themes running through this speech—our country's historical roots and its current dedication to preserve liberty, the duties of citizens of the United States, power, and human rights. They are all eloquently expressed. You would find it difficult, if not impossible, however, to rephrase any of the passages in this speech into an argument reasoning from premises to a conclusion. The entire speech is rhetoric.

In our analysis of argumentative texts, when an author also uses rhetoric, we will focus on how the two forms of rhetoric that appeal to emotions, feelings, or shared values, or to the credibility or reputation of the writer are related to the author's argument. Rhetorical statements, questions, and passages can (a) add deeper and richer meaning to the premises or conclusion of an argument, and so in that way infuse and clarify the meaning of the terms of the argument, (b) may obscure the meaning of an argument, (c) be intended to emphasize or minimize some part of an argument, or (d) be entirely extraneous to the argument. When you see a rhetorical statement, question, or passage in an argumentative text, ask yourself, why does the author employ rhetoric and not a declarative statement? What is she trying to communicate that would not be communicated at all or not as richly in a declarative sentence?

We will explore rhetoric further in chapter 7. For now, you should be aware that uses of rhetoric that appeal to emotions, feelings, or shared values, or to the credibility or reputation of the writer or speaker are different from arguments. Colloquially, they appeal to and engage the heart, not the head.

You now know the difference between argumentative texts and four other types of nonfiction texts that do not assert arguments. While these five types of nonfiction texts are generally distinct, that is not always the case. In fact, any one of these other types of writing can be used to assert an argument. To consider just one example, an explanation can be put in the form of an argument, as in this inductive argument:

The victim was shot twelve times.
None of those shots was immediately fatal.
The man did not receive medical attention for five hours after the shooting.
Anyone who is shot twelve times and does not die immediately and does not receive prompt medical attention usually bleeds to death.
We conclude that the victim likely bled to death.

This is both an explanation of the man's death and an argument that loss of blood was the cause and not something else.

We have covered a lot of ground in this chapter. So, it is useful to take a moment to summarize what we have discussed here. In sum, we did a deeper dive into the essential characteristics of an argument: by showing that two common views of arguments are incorrect (the first section); by distinguishing arguments that purport to prove their conclusions as a matter of necessity (deductive arguments) from those that only claim that their conclusions are probably true (inductive arguments) (the second section); by showing the relationship between deductive and inductive arguments and the other two major types of arguments, namely, practical and theoretical (also in the second section); by discussing how to determine which arguments successfully prove their conclusions (valid and strong arguments) and which arguments do not (invalid or weak arguments) (the third section); by examining a common argument form in which one or more of the essential premises is missing (enthymemes, in the fourth section); and by distinguishing nonfiction texts that assert arguments from four other types of nonfiction texts that do not (in the final section).

Why did we discuss these subjects in depth? The concepts discussed in this chapter are essential tools that you can and should use to better understand the meaning of any argumentative text. And, when you first approach a nonfiction text, they will allow you to determine whether the author is trying to communicate meaning through an argument at all, or whether she is engaged in a different form of nonfiction writing. To accomplish your goals in any activity, you need "the right tools for the job." You can read and struggle through many argumentative texts without these basic concepts. You are far more likely to be successful in your "job" of better understanding by grasping these "right tools" and mastering them through repeated use.

NOTES

1. James S. Miller, *The Real World Reader*, p. 30 (New York: Oxford U. Press, 2016) ("a thesis is by its very nature subjective and debatable.").

2. This view of arguments is derived from the ancient Greek philosopher Aristotle, in his treatise on arguments, *Posterior Analytics*, Book 1.

3. Lewis Vaughn, *Concise Guide to Critical Thinking*, pp. 6–7 (New York: Oxford U. Press, 2018).

4. For more examples, see ibid.

5. Reasoning by analogy has this general form:

> A is like (or is similar to) B because both have characteristics 1, 2, 3 (maybe more or fewer).
> A also has characteristic 4.
> Therefore, B likely has characteristic 4.

The more properties that A and B share, the more likely it is that they also share some other, additional property. The more A and B are alike, the stronger the reasoning from the known properties of both A and B to the unknown properties of B.

6. *Hoyle's Rules of Games*, p. 176 (New York: New American Library, 1983, Albert H. Morehead, Geoffrey Mott-Smith, eds.).

7. Robert Gerach, *General Relativity from A to B*, p. ix (Chicago: U. Chicago Press, 1978).

8. The full text is available at Our Documents—Transcript of President John F. Kennedy's Inaugural Address (1961) and many other online resources.

Chapter 5

Every Person Has a Skeleton, Every Argument Has a Structure

A capacity, and taste, for reading gives access to whatever has already been discovered by others. It is the key, or one of the keys, to the already solved problems. And not only so. It gives a relish, and facility, for successfully pursuing the unsolved ones.—Abraham Lincoln (September 30, 1859, address before the Wisconsin State Agricultural Society)

More than two thousand years ago, the Greek philosopher Aristotle wrote that the plot of every piece of literature has a beginning, middle, and an end.[1] That insight may seem pretty obvious to you, but apparently it was not obvious to his audience in ancient Athens. In any event, Aristotle's simple truth gives us a tool for better understanding argumentative texts.

For our purposes, the most useful way to think of Aristotle's insight is this: virtually every argumentative text—whether it is an article, essay, book, historical account, or something else—has an introduction, a middle, and a conclusion. ("Virtually every" is intended to flag that there may be rare exceptions to this proposition.) As the term "introduction" suggests, the introduction usually comes at or near the beginning of the work. In the most rigorous argumentative pieces, it typically does two things—it includes a statement of the author's thesis and tells the reader the plan of the work, how generally she is going to prove her thesis. The middle is where she actually does what she said she was going to do in the introduction, including putting forth the proof of her thesis. The conclusion summarizes the work and sometimes offers additional insights as to why her conclusions are important or what consequences they have for further research or action. In other words, a well-organized argumentative essay will have each of these three parts, and, ideally, the introduction will tell its readers what the essay is going to prove and how.

These three parts are the most general structure or form of an argumentative work. A rough analogy would be to a general architectural sketch of a building. You know from this sketch that the architect is designing a house (and not a movie theater, church, bridge, or boat) and how the rooms in the house are going to be arranged, their size and shape, and whether the house has a garage or not.

The goal in this chapter is to begin at the beginning—by discussing common types of introductions. One benefit of focusing on various types of introductions is that if you cannot find some form of introduction in a text, it should raise the question in your mind whether you really are reading an argumentative text.

INTRODUCTIONS—THEY COME IN VARIOUS SHAPES AND FORMS

From the perspective of understanding the argument in an argumentative text, some introductions do a whole lot of the work for you. They explicitly state the thesis of the work and how the author is going to prove it, step-by-step. Other introductions require a bit more work, and still others require that you roll up your sleeves and ask yourself, "What is this essay (or book or article) about?" Here we will examine six commonly used types of introductions. These six are not exhaustive of all possible types of introductions you will encounter. There is no such comprehensive list. Knowing these six provides you with the essential elements of introductions, and that is enough to get you started dealing with these and the others you will read. In discussing these types of introductions, we will note how some of are designed to communicate meaning in addition to that which is communicated in the bare bones of the argument itself.

HERE IS THE DESTINATION AND THE ROAD MAP TO GET THERE

In the easiest case, from the perspective of understanding the author's argument, the author's introduction expressly states what she is trying to prove in her text and the major points she is going to make to prove it. The introduction in effect says, "here's the destination (my thesis) and here's the map to show you how I'm going to get there (the plan or structure of my argument)." Her introduction may look like this:

- In this paper, I will show that X is true.

- X may stand for propositions such as:
  - God exists, or
  - the cause of World War I was extreme nationalism in Europe, or
  - extreme poverty in Africa can be reduced by 50 percent by eliminating governmental corruption, or
  - being a vegetarian will make you happy.
- In section I, I begin to demonstrate this by . . .
  - presenting facts or data, or
  - interpreting a text, or
  - refuting the position of someone who does not believe X, or
  - analyzing a concept (e.g., the concept of existence), or
  - making a moral or legal argument.
- In section II, I will . . . (whatever the next step of the argument is).
- In section III, I show . . . (whatever the next step of the argument is).
- In my conclusion in section IV, I will summarize my arguments, and show that they point to the need for future research into some point related to X or further action of type Y.[2]

The statement, "I will show (or prove or demonstrate) that X" is the author's *thesis*. In sections 1 through 3, the author would present her arguments in support of the thesis. These arguments may rely on data, quotes from other authors, analyses of concepts, refutations of the arguments made by writers who hold opposing views, or whatever else she has promised in her introduction. She would then have a concluding section wrapping it all up and maybe saying something about why the conclusion is important, what consequences it may have for future research or action, or the like. For ease of reference, from here on, we will refer to this as the "Road Map" model of an introduction.

Here is a good example of a Road Map introduction in a modern book about political and economic inequality. Because there is so much talk today about equality and inequality, this is the sort of book you may be asked to read in a political science course or a course on modern American politics. This introduction contains ellipses (. . .) to reflect editing that makes the point more apparent.

> Step by step and debate by debate, America's public officials have rewritten the rules of American politics and the American economy in ways that have benefited the few at the expense of the many. . . .
>
> Our story unfolds in three parts. Part 1 delves into the mystery of the winner-take-all economy. We come face-to-face with what has really happened in the American marketplace over the last generation: who's won and who's

lost . . . and how government has played an integral role in creating these new economic realities. . . .

Part 2 takes us down to the subterranean roots of the winner-take-all economy, which lie . . . in the political transformations of the 1970s.

In part 3, we provide a portrait of the new world of American politics forged in this crucible—the world of "Winner-Take-All Politics." We do so through the prism of the nation's two political parties, showing how Republicans and Democrats have both responded, in different ways, to the political pull of the superrich.[3]

The first sentence states the authors' thesis, what they are going to prove. The next three paragraphs lay out the road map of how they are going to prove it. The beauty of this sort of introduction is that it directs the reader to the essential elements of the authors' argument point by point. With this introduction, you would be able to (re)state the authors' thesis and then use the "part 1, part 2, and part 3" structure, and the main argument under each of these parts, to reconstruct the principal elements of the argument of the book.

Consider this very clear Road Map introduction from a sociological study on crime, and specifically on lethal violence, in the United States. Again, this introduction has been edited, as shown by the ellipses (. . .) to make the point more apparent.

This study will demonstrate that lethal violence is a specific problem separate from general crime rates. The first five chapters of the book will present the available evidence on crime and lethal violence in the United States. The second part of the book will then examine how changing the subject from crime generally to lethal violence specifically can improve our understanding of the effects of factors such as guns, mass media, and drugs. . . .

The third part of this book addresses the question of how governmental policies might be redesigned to reduce the volume of intentional injury and death in the United States. . . .

So, the first segment of the book establishes the factual foundation for concluding that lethal violence is a central problem in contemporary American life. The second section shows some implications of the pattern established in Part I on our understanding of the causes of deadly violence. The third section then considers strategies of harm prevention.[4]

The first sentence of the first paragraph clearly states the thesis of the book, namely, "This study will demonstrate that lethal violence is a specific problem separate from general crime rates." The remaining sentences in the first paragraph and the following two paragraphs tell you, in broad terms, how the authors are going to prove this thesis. You cannot reconstruct the argument of the book from this Road Map introduction, but you do know how the authors intend to present their argument.

So now you know what an ideal introduction looks like from the perspective of understanding an author's thesis and how he intends to prove it. Note that the examples above are from books. You are more likely to find the Road Map introduction in a book than in a short essay or opinion piece in a magazine or newspaper. Because the thread (the elements) of the argument is more readily lost in a book of several hundred pages, there is more need to set forth the plan of the argument for the reader in such a work than in a much shorter essay or opinion piece in the mass media.

That said, there is a catch. In academic writing, and even more so in popular essays for a mass audience, this sort of complete and clear Road Map introduction is not as common as we might like or expect. Many introductions in scholarly argumentative texts do not provide you with a complete road map. Academic introductions often do not start with the thesis and generally do not outline each step of their proofs. Essays in the mass media do this even less often. Argumentative texts are not always written with the goal of making the reader's reading easy. Sometimes road maps—even electronic road maps on your smartphones and other devices—are only partially complete, missing some critical streets or landmarks, or frayed at the edges (missing information). Introductions are no different. Let's consider two examples of incomplete Road Map introductions to illustrate the point.

In "Justice and Equality" David A. J. Richards provides us with a good example of the sort of incomplete introduction you are likely to find in an academic essay. Again, the text includes ellipses (. . .) and brackets ([]) which reflect edits to the text. These devices make the passage clearer to readers who have not studied any political philosophy (presumably, almost all of you). This editing does not in any way affect the point the example is designed to illustrate.

> Since the earliest philosophical reflection on the concept of justice . . ., justice has been supposed to involve or implicate the idea of equality. . . . In this essay, I try to explain the formal idea of justice which appears to unite all serious philosophical reflection on the idea, and then to focus on two levels of disagreement about how the underlying idea of equality should be interpreted—first, [and so on], and second, [and so on]. Finally, I turn to the implications of the philosophical disagreements for the understanding of various substantive controversies over issues of justice.[5]

Read this introduction again. Is something missing?

Yes—where is the thesis? Richards has given us a road map—he tells us what the major road markers are. The road map is as clear as we could hope for—(1) he will begin by explaining the "formal idea of justice," (2) he next discusses two disagreements about the idea of equality tied to that idea of justice, and (3) he wraps up with a discussion of the implications of his analysis in steps (1) and (2).

Great road map, but what is the destination? What is his thesis? Richards does not tell us what he is going to prove. In the second sentence, he tells us that he will "try to explain the formal idea of justice which appears to unite all serious philosophical reflection on the idea." So far, so good. But that does not tell us what that "formal idea of justice" is, what he means by this phrase, what he is trying to prove regarding that concept, or what premises he will offer to support his thesis about "the formal idea of justice." You need to read the rest of his (very good) essay to get answers to these questions.

One more example of an incomplete Road Map introduction, this one from Sigmund Freud, the father of modern psychology. Chapter I of Freud's classic *The Interpretation of Dreams* begins with this paragraph:

> In the pages that follow I shall bring forward proof that there is a psychological technique which makes it possible to interpret dreams, and that, if that procedure is employed, every dream reveals itself as a psychical structure which has a meaning and which can be inserted at an assignable point in the mental activities of waking life. I shall further endeavor to elucidate the processes to which the strangeness and obscurity of dreams are due and to deduce from those processes the nature of psychical forces by whose concurrent or mutually opposing action dreams are generated. Having gone thus far, my description will break off, for it will have reached a point at which the problem of dreams merges into more comprehensive problems, the solution of which must be approached upon the basis of material of another kind.

That paragraph is tough sledding! Unless you have studied a lot of Freud's works, or a lot of psychology generally, you probably do not understand the first sentence (or perhaps anything in the rest of the paragraph, for that matter). Do not worry about that.

The good news is that you do not need to understand it for our purposes. The point to focus on here is that there is no doubt that the first sentence is a statement of Freud's thesis. He is telling us flat out—"I'm going to prove to you that there is a technique that can be used to interpret dreams" and so on. In the second sentence, he tells us—"There's more! I'm also going to prove to you the causes of dreams and the implications of those causes." And in the third sentence, he tells us, in effect, "anything beyond those first two tasks gets me too far into other matters, so I'm not going to deal with them."

That paragraph is a good a statement of the thesis (or, perhaps more accurately, two theses, the first and second sentences) and the general plan of this work. It is as direct and clear as you are likely to find in academic writing. But Freud does not get three cheers for that. He gets about one and a half cheers. His first chapter provides no further detailed statement of how he is going to prove his thesis or what the processes are which he refers to in the second sentence. For that, you need to look at the book's detailed table of contents and skim through the early paragraphs of each chapter. The point, in short, is that this is a good start to being a complete Road Map introduction, because he clearly states his thesis (or theses). But he does not provide the road map that he is using to get to this destination. You could not use this introduction to outline the main elements of his argument, even in a very general fashion.

Any actual introduction you encounter in an argumentative text may deviate from the Road Map model in various ways, and to a greater or lesser extent. If you are aware of this, you will have greater confidence in your reading of a text because you will be aware that if you are confused, unclear, or puzzled, that may well be a result of how the author has written his introduction, and what he has omitted from that introduction. Your confusion may not be the result of your lack of knowledge or familiarity with the subject matter you are reading about. If an author has provided you with his thesis and all of the elements of his argument (the road map) and you still do not understand what he is saying, well, do not be discouraged. Just roll up your sleeves and be prepared to do some work figuring it out.

THE SUBJECT VARIATION ON THE ROAD MAP

The Road Map introduction has a close cousin, which we will refer to here as the "Subject Variation" on the Road Map. In this form, the author does not state his thesis, but rather tells you what the subject of his essay (or speech) is and the manner in which he is going to discuss it.[6] He replaces a statement of his thesis with a statement of the subject of his essay and then may also provide you with a sketch of how he is going to discuss this subject.

Debates about equality often set up an opposition between equality and another value, especially the values of liberty or excellence. This is not new. In the early 1960s, John W. Gardner wrote a short book titled, *Excellence, Can We Be Equal and Excellent Too?* The "Introduction" to this book is a nice example of the Subject Variation.

> The subject [of equality] has never ceased to interest me. This is a book about excellence, more particularly about the conditions under which excellence is possible in our kind of society; but it is also—inevitably—a book about equality, about the kinds of equality that can and must be honored, and the kinds that cannot be forced.[7]

Mr. Gardner does not state a thesis or set forth a road map with the plan of his book. He does make clear, however, that excellence is the subject of his book, and also, "inevitably," equality. This is a good example of the Subject Variation.

The Subject Variation introduction is incomplete from the perspective of understanding the author's argument because there is no statement of the author's thesis and how he intends to prove it. Your reading of argumentative texts will benefit by being attuned to that. At a minimum, you will be less frustrated when your reading is not going smoothly. You will know that sometimes reading a difficult text is like driving a car with bad shocks over a bumpy, dirt road. There is nothing you can do but try to figure out how best to get to your destination with what the author has given you.

Now, to mix things up just a bit, sometimes an author will introduce his work with *both* the Road Map model *and* the Subject Variation. That is, he will both state the thesis *and* the subject of the work, and follow those statements with a more or less clear exposition of the plan of the text or how he or she will prove the thesis.

A good example of this dual strategy is found in John Stuart Mill's classic treatise *On Liberty* (written in 1859). Mill's very first sentence in this text states:

> The subject of this essay is not the so-called "liberty of the will," so unfortunately opposed to the misnamed doctrine of philosophical necessity; but civil, or social liberty: the nature and limits of the power which can be legitimately exercised by society over the individual.[8]

Wow. Here is a single sentence with two commas, a semicolon, and a colon. Your high school writing or composition teacher would have given this sentence a poor grade. This statement of the subject of *On Liberty* is not eloquent, it is difficult to read, and it is not even good sentence structure by today's standards.

Nonetheless, if you read the sentence carefully (and repeatedly), you know that Mill is going to write about the scope of "civil or social liberty" in modern society (his subject). As he further explains this idea, he is going to write about the "nature and limits of the power" which a society can legitimately exercise over any one person to constrain that individual's liberty (or freedom).

Having stated the subject, a few paragraphs later, Mill states his thesis:

> The object of this essay is to assert one very simple principle, as entitled to govern absolutely the dealings of society with the individual in the way of compulsion and control, whether the means be used be physical force in the form of legal penalties or the moral coercion of public opinion. That principle is that the sole end for which mankind are warranted, individually or collectively, in interfering with the liberty of action of any of their number is self-protection.

> That the only purpose for which power can be rightfully exercised over any member of a civilized community, against his will, is to prevent harm to others.[9]

You will seldom find a clearer, more self-conscious statement of a thesis than this. Note Mill's use of the term "object" (i.e., the purpose or goal) in the first sentence. That is usually a clear tip-off that what follows is the author's thesis. *When an author uses "the object," "the point," "the purpose," "the goal," or "the end" of my essay (or book, or article, etc.) is . . ."* that is the point he is trying to prove—his thesis.

After a few more paragraphs in which he elaborates on the meaning of the thesis, Mill then provides a statement of part of his plan to prove the thesis:

> It will be convenient for the argument if, instead of at once entering upon the general thesis, we confine ourselves in the first instance to a single branch of it on which the principle here stated is, if not fully, yet to a certain point, recognized by the current opinions. This one branch is the Liberty of Thought, from which it is impossible to separate the cognate liberty of speaking and writing.[10]

Mill does not expressly tell us in his introduction how he is going to prove his thesis. He only offers some general remarks suggesting the main premises of his argument. Similarly, he only offers some general suggestions as to the other realms of liberty he is going to discuss in addition to liberty of thought and speech.

Nonetheless, for our purposes, the salient point of Mill's introduction is: the introduction contains both (a) a statement of a thesis and a *partial* plan of his essay and (b) a statement of the subject of the essay (the proper scope of individual liberty in modern society). Now, these two options are not always mutually exclusive; one does not necessarily exclude the other. They are alternative ways to tell the reader what a text is about and how the author is going to prove his point. They are often complementary. Note, once again: sometimes introductions are incomplete from a purely logical or argumentative perspective, even in the work of a great philosopher like Mill.

It is worth repeating: you will not find the ideal Road Map introduction in many academic essays and will find it even less frequently in articles written for a mass audience. Most introductions do not usually tell you the destination is the Emerald City and give you a road map brighter and straighter than the Yellow Brick Road. That is okay. Reading would get pretty boring very quickly if everything you read had the same format. You do not want to listen to the same music all the time. Sometimes Taylor Swift, sometimes Ariana Grande or Adele, and sometimes even a bit of Bach or Debussy.

ASKING A QUESTION (STATING A PROBLEM)

One common way for an author to introduce an argumentative writing or speech is by asking a question or posing a problem, and then telling you that he will answer it. How many times have you heard this from a politician or other public speaker—"What is the biggest problem America faces today? Well, I'll tell you what it is, my fellow Americans. It's . . ." Or, more particularly, "Can America afford a $15 minimum wage? Of course it can. Let's look at what three prominent economists say."

Here are two extended examples of this type of introduction, one from a modern philosopher and one from an ancient philosopher. In the late twentieth century, the philosopher Joel Feinberg wrote:

> What is it to deserve something? This guileless question can hardly fail to trouble the reflective person who ponders it. Yet until its peculiar perplexities are resolved, a full understanding of the nature of justice is impossible, for surely the concepts of justice and desert are closely connected. This essay has as its ulterior purpose the illumination of that connection; its direct aim is analysis of the concept of personal desert.[11]

Clearly, Feinberg is writing an essay that will analyze the concept of desert (or personal desert). He does not tell us in the very first paragraph how he is going to do that, but we do know from this paragraph that he thinks it is a perplexing concept that requires philosophical analysis.

Consider, next, an introduction from the fifth century BCE, by the Greek philosopher Plato:

> Can you tell me, Socrates, whether virtue is acquired by teaching or by practice; or if neither by teaching nor practice, then whether it comes to man by nature, or in what other way?[12]

Plato, like Feinberg, does not explicitly tell us that the rest of the work is going to be devoted to answering the question posed. Some things are implied in any writing. Plato does not say this because he assumes that you know that he would not have asked the question at the beginning of the book if he did not intend to answer it, or at least explore it.

Dr. Martin Luther King Jr.'s sermon "Antidotes for fear" provides another example of this form of introduction. It is especially instructive because the sermon begins by stating one problem, shows that problem to be unsolvable, and then proceeds to state and discuss a related, but different, problem. (The complete sermon is attached at Appendix E of the companion *Workbook for Reading Argumentative Texts*.)

The introduction begins:

> In these days of catastrophic change and calamitous uncertainty, is there any man who does not experience the depression and bewilderment of crippling fear, which, like a nagging hound of hell, pursues our every footstep?[13]

In the following eight paragraphs of the introduction, Dr. King discusses and answers this question by concluding, "Our problem is not to be rid of fear but rather to harness and master it." Having begun his sermon by stating (in highly rhetorical terms) the problem that fear is an inescapable emotion that haunts everyone, Dr. King concludes his introduction by telling us that the remainder of his sermon will answer a different, related problem: "How may it be mastered?"

By starting his introduction with one question and ending it with another, Dr. King is saying, in effect, "you may think that the problem is how to rid yourself of fear, but it's really how to master fear; so, I am going to speak about *that* problem." We will discuss this introduction a bit more below.

One final example of this sort of introduction is instructive. Here is the first paragraph of Hyman Gross's essay "Privacy and Autonomy," which is edited slightly for brevity and clarity.

> Why is privacy desirable? When is its loss objectionable and when is it not? How much privacy is a person entitled to? . . . Seldom is privacy considered as the condition under which there is *control* over acquaintance with one's personal affairs by the one enjoying it. I wish here to show how consideration of privacy in this neglected aspect is helpful in answering the basic questions [asked above]. First I shall attempt to make clear this part of the idea of privacy, next suggest why privacy in this aspect merits protection, then argue that some important dilemmas are less vexing when we do get clear about these things, and finally offer a cautionary remark regarding the relation of privacy and autonomy.[14]

Note here how Gross's introduction clearly states his thesis and then gives you the road map on how he will prove it. His thesis is: "I wish to show here how consideration of privacy in this neglected aspect is helpful in answering the basic questions [asked above]." And here are the three big markers in his road map; I have added the bracketed comments to make the last three markers obvious: "First I shall attempt to make clear this part of the idea of privacy, [second] next suggest why privacy in this aspect merits protection, then [third] argue that some important dilemmas are less vexing when we do get clear about these things, and [fourth] finally offer a cautionary remark regarding the relation of privacy and autonomy."

Note also how easily Gross's introduction could be rewritten to conform to the Road Map model of an introduction discussed above. Here is what it would look like if rewritten in that fashion:

> I wish here to show how consideration of privacy as the condition under which there is *control* over acquaintance with one's personal affairs by the one enjoying it is helpful in answering three basic questions: (1) Why is privacy desirable? (2) When is its loss objectionable and when is it not? (3) How much privacy is a person entitled to? To show this I shall, first, attempt to make clear this part of the idea of privacy; second, suggest why privacy in this aspect merits protection; third, argue that some important dilemmas are less vexing when we do get clear about these things; and finally offer a cautionary remark regarding the relation of privacy and autonomy.

The first sentence is his thesis and the second sentence is his road map.

Gross's introduction is better stylistically than this rewritten version of it. At the very least, it has the advantage of not taxing the reader's attention with the very long sentences in the rewritten version. You may have noticed that *in their content* these two versions are identical. But ask yourself—is any meaning gained or lost in the rewritten version of Gross's introduction? We will answer that question momentarily.

This rewriting of Gross's introduction provides a nice illustration of a critical point in reading for understanding. *If you do not understand an introduction that takes a form other than the Road Map model, try rewriting it to conform to that model.* You may find that your confusion or lack of understanding is a result of the author's omitting an express statement of the thesis (like David A. J. Richards did with his introduction) or some critical parts of the road map (as Freud did in the example above).

When you encounter either of those omissions, flagging them for yourself allows you to do two things: (1) ask the question, "who's confused or unclear here—me or the author?" (hint: it is not always you) and (2) read the rest of the text with a focused attention on what sorts of information or statements you need to clear up the confusion.

Gross's statement of his thesis and the four steps he is going to take to prove it are broad and general, but that is okay. He has told you what blanks he will fill in later in the body of the essay. When an author does *not* do that for you, it *may be* a red flag that he is not clear about what he really wants to prove or how he is going to prove it. This is only a possibility, and is not necessarily so. You need to read on to determine if it is style or substance that has led to the omissions.

As you read in chapter 1, a central objective of this book is to discuss how to understand the meaning of an argumentative text, recognizing that such meaning is to be found in the elements of the argument itself and in the other components of the work in which the argument is found. Accordingly, this is a good place to pause and ask what additional meaning, if any, does an author communicate when she introduces her work with a question or set of related questions, as contrasted to those introductions that simply state the thesis or the subject and how the author intends to prove the thesis or discuss the subject? There are several possible answers to this question, and some of them depend on how the author has asked the question in her introduction. Here are three principal answers.

First, one way to think of an argumentative text (and perhaps the best way, but we do not need to prove that here) is that every thesis is an attempt to answer a question or solve a problem. If we all knew the nature of justice, equality, or desert, no one would need to go to all of the trouble of writing an essay that states, for example, "I will prove to you that justice is giving each person what she deserves," or the like. So, stating the question that the thesis is intended to answer (a) can frame the scope of the discussion and its conclusion and (b) is often a good way of focusing the reader on the importance of the topic in the first instance.

Plato's question, "Can you tell me, Socrates, whether virtue is acquired by teaching or by practice; or if neither by teaching nor practice, then whether it comes to man by nature, or in what other way?" is an example of (a); it tells us that the issue he is concerned with is how a person becomes or is virtuous, and not primarily on the nature of virtue itself. Feinberg's question about desert—"What is it to deserve something?"—is an example of (b), which he reinforces in the next sentence, "This guileless question can hardly fail to trouble the reflective person who ponders it."

Second, the prefatory context for a question can communicate a meaning and importance of the question that a mere flat statement of it cannot. A few pages above we saw that Dr. King began his introduction to "Antidotes for fear" with this question:

> In these days of catastrophic change and calamitous uncertainty, is there any man who does not experience the depression and bewilderment of crippling fear, which, like a nagging hound of hell, pursues our every footstep?

Once Dr. King has grabbed his congregation's attention with this highly rhetorical question and given his listeners reasons to believe that none of us can rid ourselves of fear altogether, he then concludes his introduction by stating, "Our problem is not to be rid of fear but rather to harness and master it. How may it be mastered?" Dr. King then devotes the remainder of his sermon to answering this second question.

Suppose Dr. King began his sermon with this second question—"how may [fear] be mastered?" In that case, he would have invited this response from many in his congregation, "Master it? Heck, I want to be rid of it altogether." So, in order to dismiss that thought, and to have his congregation understand that his second question is the one they ought to focus on in their everyday lives, he begins his sermon by asking the first question and answering it by showing that fear is inescapable. Once he has done that, the practical importance of mastering fear, and the techniques he recommends to do this, are all the greater.

Finally, the manner in which an author asks a question, or set of questions, can be a way of telling his readers that they have not been thinking of a problem in the right way, not framing it properly. Recall Gross's three questions: "Why is privacy desirable? When is its loss objectionable and when is it not? How much privacy is a person entitled to?" After asking these three questions, Gross follows them by his statement of his thesis, "Seldom is privacy considered as the condition under which there is *control* over acquaintance with one's personal affairs by the one enjoying it." This stylistic maneuver communicates that there are three interrelated problems and they have a common solution.

As Gross has written his introduction, he is saying, "Heads up. If you think these are three separate questions, each requiring a different answer, think again; I am going to prove to you they are interrelated and have a common solution, namely, that privacy is a condition under which . . ." This meaning arguably is conveyed in my rewriting of Gross's introduction, but if it is, it is communicated less powerfully and with less impact.

Many argumentative texts, especially academic articles and essays, begin with the statement of a problem that the essay is intended to solve. You will have greater ease in understanding these texts if you become familiar with this form of introduction. This is particularly true given that the statement of a question often makes certain assumptions that are disputable or the formulation of the problem may be itself confused. When Plato asks whether virtue is acquired by teaching, practice, or whether it comes to a person naturally, he would appear to be assuming that we know what virtue is. To see why this is a big assumption, take some time to debate the question "what is virtue?" with your friends.

THE ANECDOTAL INTRODUCTION

One very common way to begin an argumentative essay is to tell a brief story, an anecdote. This is a style often seen in editorials or other essays in the mass media. If you want to grab an audience's attention, a tried-and-true method is to tell a gripping story.

Consider this introduction from a *Newsweek* article entitled, "Guns in America, What Must Be Done":

> After it was over, after the SWAT teams had swept in and the suspect had fled, after the screams and the tears, a little boy too young to know his letters wanted to thank the men who rescued him from the shooter. Handing a green crayon and a piece of blue construction paper, four-and-a-half-year-old Nathan Powers started dictating, "thank you policemen," Nathan said, "for saving us from the gun because you're our friend."[15]

The article then proceeds to describe a shooting and hostage situation in a Jewish Community Center outside of Los Angeles which occurred a few days earlier, proceeds from that incident to a broader discussion of gun violence in America, and then offers certain prescriptions for what must be done to end the violence.

Let's consider a second example. There is a long-standing question at the heart of the Judeo-Christian religious tradition, which is sometimes referred to as the problem of evil or the problem of suffering. The question is: if God is all-powerful (omnipotent) and all-good (omnibenevolent), why is there so much evil (or suffering) in the world? There are many books and essays on the topic.[16] Here is how one author uses a series of anecdotes to introduce his essay on this topic in a *New York Times* essay, which I have edited a bit in the interest of brevity:

> Last month I checked in on a childhood friend whose 13-year old son committed suicide last year after struggling with a brain injury. He told me, "I've stopped crying every day, which is a major transition." . . . Another lifelong friend recently died of colon cancer. . . . Two weeks ago I spoke to a friend whose wife had told him she no longer wanted to be married to him because of his relapse into alcoholism, which he described as a "deep, dark struggle" that robbed him of his true personality.[17]

After this series of anecdotes, and many more paragraphs of context, the author states his version of the problem of suffering, "So what, then, does Christianity have to offer in the midst of hardships and heartache?" and his answer to that question, his thesis, is, "The answer, I think, is consolation, including the consolation that comes from being a part of a Christian community."

People like to learn through a good story. Politicians know this; Lincoln was a master storyteller. Lawyers use stories when they are arguing to a jury because for a lay audience a story is a far more effective way to communicate a point of view than a dry recitation of facts. Editors of mass media publications know this too, and so you see many essays and opinion pieces introduced through anecdotes.[18]

It is instructive to press the point a bit further. Why are the anecdotes in these two examples powerful? What do they communicate to the reader that a more theoretical or abstract discussion of gun violence or the suffering many people experience would not?

Notice these two features: (1) they are very realistic stories and (2) they have enough detail, enough particularity, to make them persuasive and credible. In the synagogue shooting example, consider the difference in the meaning conveyed by the paragraph quoted above and this simple, generic, factual statement, "One child who was in the synagogue expressed his gratitude to the police after the incident." In the article on suffering, consider the difference between the paragraph quoted and a plain, generic, factual statement like this, "We all know people who have suffered from various causes." If you were to outline these articles, these two plain, generic, factual restatements of these anecdotes may have a place. But they do not convey, as the anecdotes do, the complete experience in a way that causes us to react, "yes, I can imagine being there, seeing this happening; I could have heard those words."

When an anecdotal introduction is used because of its rhetorical force, it likely will not contain statements that are either premises of or a conclusion to an argument. Nonetheless, such an introduction may add meaning to or obscure the meaning of the terms of an argument. Careful analysis of the relationship of the anecdote and the argument in the text is required to determine what the author is trying to communicate.

LET'S GET RIGHT TO THE POINT

In this form of introduction, the author does not lay out a road map to an extended argument, because there is no extended argument, and space (or time, in the case of a speech) is in short supply. Rather, the author typically states a thesis and then gets right to proving it. A few examples serve to illustrate this type of introduction.

In November 1872, Susan B. Anthony, the suffragist, was arrested for illegally voting in the presidential election. The next year she embarked on a speaking tour, during which she delivered a short speech entitled, "Women's Right to Vote." This is her entire introduction:

> Friends and fellow citizens: I stand before you tonight under indictment for the alleged crime of having voted at the last presidential election, without having a lawful right to vote. It shall be my work this evening to prove to you that in

thus voting, I not only committed no crime, but, instead, simply exercised my citizen's rights, guaranteed to me and all United States citizens by the National Constitution, beyond the power of any state to deny.[19]

The first sentence after the greeting provides the necessary context (I was indicted in a criminal court . . .). The second sentence jumps right to Ms. Anthony's thesis: "It shall be my work this evening to prove to you that in thus voting, I not only committed no crime . . ." Ms. Anthony offers no road map as to how she is going to prove this thesis. Rather, she immediately proceeds to set forth her proof of the thesis by quoting the entire preamble to the United States Constitution and then, in the following paragraphs, interpreting the preamble as granting her and all other women the right to vote.

You commonly see this form of introduction in very short articles or essays, such as newspaper editorials. In an editorial appearing a few weeks after the 2016 presidential election, discussing President-elect Trump's reaction to the recount sought by the candidate of the Green Party in three states, the *Tampa Bay Times* editorial board wrote:

> President-elect Donald Trump is railing against the very system that will put him in the White House. Without any substantiation, the man who will be President went on a Twitter rant this weekend, saying that he would have "won the popular vote if you deduct the millions of people who voted illegally." This is a baseless assertion that undermines the faith that Americans have in their system of free and fair elections. PolitiFact.com gives it a false rating of "Pants on Fire."[20]

Quick, before you read on, which sentence is the thesis?

Here, the thesis is found in the third sentence, not in the first. After this introductory paragraph, the editorial then proceeds to discuss the recount process, the popular votes in the three states in which the recounts were being sought, and its participants.

JUST THE FACTS, MA'AM, JUST THE FACTS

Throughout most of the 1950s, there was a weekly detective show on television called *Dragnet*, starring Jack Webb as the lead detective, "Joe Friday." Friday was a very watered-down, bland, TV version of a detective. Quite commonly, when Friday was questioning a woman witness whose version of events wandered off into her gripes or opinions, he would stop her with the admonition, "Just the facts, ma'am, just the facts . . ."

Some introductions are like that—just the facts. You see this often in introductions to sociological or criminological studies. Here is an example:

> Approximately 20,000 persons are murdered in the United States each year, making homicide the eleventh leading cause of death and the sixth leading cause of the loss of potential years of life before age sixty-five. In the United States between 1960 and 1980, the death rate from homicide by means other than firearms increased by 85 percent. In contrast, the death rate from homicide by firearms during this same period increased by 160 percent.[21]

You cannot get a much more factual, more data-thick, introduction than that. Why would the author introduce his article by reciting these facts?

Often the author is producing a series of facts in order to frame a problem, to tell you that he conducted an empirical study of the problem, and to present the results of the study. This may look very factual, data-driven, and value- and opinion-neutral. Often enough it is. Facts, data, and statistics can be manipulated, however, and so when you are reading what claims to be a "scientific" or "purely empirical" study, you need to ask yourself if the author is really being or trying to be scientific and objective or whether he has an agenda hiding behind well-selected facts.

Much more could be said about this form of introduction, but it suffices here that you are aware of it and the contexts in which you are likely to encounter it.

To summarize, an ideal introduction from the prospective of presenting the argument of a text will state the author's thesis and the plan by which she is going to prove her thesis. It may also include a statement of why the thesis is important and the implications of that thesis for future research or individual or collective action.

Introductions sometimes follow this ideal model, but more often deviate from it in one or more ways. Sometimes an introduction focuses on evoking emotions that strictly are not part of the argument or on communicating the importance of the argument itself. In other cases in which an introduction deviates from this ideal, as in certain scholarly works, it is because the author was not as rigorous as she could have been (intentionally or not), or because the author thought her readers did not need to have her argument expressly set forth point by point, or for some other reason. In any event, you now know what elements to look for in an introduction and what an author may have included or omitted. That is a big step in reading for understanding. Keep these types on introductions in mind as we analyze various texts throughout this book.

This extended discussion of introductions gives you three tools for your reading toolbox.

- *You should not expect a simple, straight-line progression of argumentation in most texts, especially texts designed for a mass audience.* Texts vary in their argumentative rigor and in their modes of presentation. Some will have easy-to-follow Road Map introductions and others will make your reading more challenging.
- *A text may lack an introduction and still be making an argument.* But when you read a text without a recognizable introduction, you should be analyzing it with an eye toward determining whether it is making an argument or whether it is one of the other types of nonargumentative, nonfiction writing that are discussed in chapter 4.
- If you are struggling to determine whether a text is asserting an argument, independent of it having or lacking a clearly stated introduction, try this. *First, step back, look at the essay as a whole, and ask yourself: what is the point of this essay? what is the crucial message the author is trying to communicate? Second, is the author trying to prove the truth of that point by reasoning from (on the basis of) other statements in the text or is he doing something else?* Your answers to these questions will allow you to determine whether the text is asserting an argument.

NOTES

1. Aristotle, *Poetics*, book II, chap. 7. Aristotle made this comment specifically about works of tragedy, but his discussion shows that he meant it to apply to any piece of literature with a plot. The former American Poet Laureate Billy Collins has turned this insight into a marvelous poem, aptly titled "Aristotle." You can find it at poetryfoundation.org/poems/46706/aristotle.

2. Many authors also will include in their introductions a statement of the importance of their thesis or the topic on which they have chosen to write. This is less common in academic writing, since the authors usually are writing for other academics who know the importance of the topic or a specific thesis.

3. Jacob S. Hacker, Paul Pierson, *Winner-Take-All Politics*, pp. 6–8 (New York: Simon & Schuster, 2010).

4. Franklin E. Zimring, Gordon Hawkins, *Crime Is Not the Problem*, pp. xi–xii (New York: Oxford U. Press 1997).

5. David A. J. Richards, "Justice and Equality," in *And Justice for All*, p. 241 (Totowa, NJ: Rowman & Littlefield 1982, Tom Regan and Donald VanDeVeer, eds.).

6. The introduction in the essay by David A. J. Richards discussed above may be read as an example of this sort of introduction, if we read his statement "I try to explain the formal idea of justice . . ." as a statement of the subject of his essay.

7. *Excellence, Can We Be Equal and Excellent Too?* p. xi (New York: Harper & Row 1962).

8. John Stuart Mill, *On Liberty*, p. 3 (Indianapolis: Bobbs-Merrill 1956).

9. *Ibid.,* p. 13.

10. *Ibid.,* p. 18.

11. Joel Feinberg, "Justice and Personal Desert," in *Doing and Deserving,* p. 55 (Princeton: Princeton University 1974). Are you confused by the term "desert"? It is one of those odd words that has three possible meanings and none of these meanings has anything to do with the others. The Sahara Desert and the Mojave Desert are dry, sandy places that get little rainfall. This type of desert (a noun) clearly is not what Professor Feinberg is discussing. A soldier can desert his unit or you can desert your friend in a moment of great need. "Desert" is that sense is a verb that means to abandon or fail. It has nothing to do with dry, sandy places, and is also not the sense Professor Feinberg means. When he talks about "desert," he means it in the sense used in these sentences: "she deserves the award" or "he didn't deserve that treatment." Very loosely, "desert" in that sense means to give someone what she is owed or to give him what is not due to him. And none of these three meanings has anything to do with "dessert," which is an entirely different word referring to all of those goodies we love to eat after a meal.

12. Plato, *Meno,* p. 23 (Indianapolis: Library of Liberal Arts 1949, trans. B. Jowett).

13. Martin Luther King Jr., "Antidotes for fear," in *Strength to Love,* p. 115 (Philadelphia: Fortress Press 1981).

14. Hyman Gross, "Privacy and Autonomy," in *Philosophy of Law,* p. 246 (Belmont, CA: Wadsworth Publishing 1980, J. Feinberg, H. Gross, eds.).

15. *Newsweek,* Aug. 23, 1999, p. 23 (reprinted in *The Gun Control Debate,* pp. 112–16). (Amherst, NY: Prometheus Books 2001, Lee Nisbet, ed.).

16. One of the most popular books in this genre is by Rabbi Harold S. Kushner, *Why Do Bad Things Happen to Good People?* (New York: Avon Books 1981).

17. Peter Wehner, "After Great Pain, Where is God?" *New York Times,* Mar. 26, 2017, p. SR10 (New York ed.), available at nytimes.com/2017/03/25/opinion/sunday/after-great-pain-where-is-god.html.

18. A note of caution: be very careful in your use of an anecdotal introduction in your argumentative term papers. Your instructor may view it as unnecessary or distracting, since you have her attention and she likely will be looking for your best arguments, not your best rhetoric.

19. Available at sourcebooks.fordham.edu/mod/1873anthony.asp. In 1873, Ms. Anthony was tried for this crime, found guilty, and fined $100, a fine which she never paid.

20. "Stop the rigged-vote stuff" (as reprinted in the *Pittsburgh Post-Gazette,* Nov. 30, 2016, p. A-9), available at post-gazette.com/opinion/2016/11/30/Stop-the-rigged-vote-stuff/stories/201611300077.

21. John Henry Sloan, et al., "Handgun Regulations, Crime, Assaults, and Homicide," in *The Gun Control Debate,* p. 315 (Amherst, NY: Prometheus Books 2001, L. Nisbet, Ph.D., ed.), reprinted from the *New Eng. J. of Medicine* 319, no. 19, pp. 1256–63 (Nov. 10, 1988).

Chapter 6

What Does the Skeleton Look Like? Outlines and Summaries

Some people think of reading only as a kind of escape: an escape from the "real" everyday world to an imaginary world, the world of books. Books are much more. They are a way of being fully human.—Susan Sontag (American essayist, novelist, and public intellectual, 1933–2004), "A Letter to Borges," in *Where the Stress Falls*, p. 112 (New York: Farrar, Straus and Giroux 2001)

By the time you finish high school and college, you will have taken many English, history, political science, sociology, criminology, or anthropology courses. Yet it is highly probable that no teacher will have taught you the importance and usefulness of outlining a writing that you do not understand, or that you partially understand but want to understand a whole lot better. That is a real shame. Outlining reveals structure. The structure of a text communicates meaning. If you do not understand the structure of a text, you will not grasp the meaning the structure conveys.

The first section of this chapter teaches you how to outline an argumentative text. The second section covers a related topic, namely, summaries. The final section asks you to step back and reflect on the utility of what you have learned in the prior two sections of this chapter.

OUTLINES

The purpose of an outline is to present the structure of a text. It sets forth:

1. the principal points (argumentative and nonargumentative) the text is making,

2. the evidence (i.e., the facts, scientific studies, anecdotes, opinions of others, analysis of concepts, and so on) that the author uses to support the main points,
3. the relationships between the points the author is making and the evidence presented to support those points, and
4. the order in which the author makes her points.

Think of an outline as the skeleton of a human body (or the blueprint of a building). It shows the frame or form that everything else is built around and the order in which the parts are joined together and follow each other.

Very few of the articles, essays, editorials, and op-ed[1] pieces you will read in the mass media follow a strict logical progression of argumentation. In other words, you almost never see anything like this: "A is true and B is true. So, I conclude that C is true." Or, equivalently, you seldom see this bare-bones form of argument:

My thesis is that [C] Socrates is mortal.
We know this because
[A] all men are mortal and
[B] Socrates is a man.

Why? Because the first rule in writing these types of pieces is not to be boring. Nobody wants to read boring stuff, at least not beyond the first paragraph or two. So, these types of texts usually sprinkle anecdotes, data, or quotes throughout the piece, often with little attention to the logical progression of the argument. These texts assert arguments, even when the premises and conclusion of the argument are scattered about.

So, in analyzing the text for its meaning you will need to determine what the argument is, what else is included in the text that is not part of the argument, why those other parts are included, and what those other parts do to the argument (make it more or less clear, give some parts additional emphasis, add emotional appeals, and so on). One of the best ways to do that is to do an outline of the piece. It is useful to see what an outline of such an essay may look like.

AN OPINION PIECE ON STUDYING LATIN

Read the essay, "Study Latin If You Want to Talk Like a supervillain," attached at Appendix A.[2] This essay initially was delivered as a short video clip during the *NewsHour* on the Public Broadcasting System (PBS), and then transcribed to the PBS website.

Okay, you are back from reading the article. Because you are just getting started learning how to outline, we begin by discussing a complete outline of the article. To make our discussion easier to follow, we will refer to the paragraphs in this article in this fashion—[Paragraph 1], [Paragraph 2], and so on.

Here is a reasonable outline of this article:

1. If you possibly can do so, you should study Latin. [Paragraph 1]
2. Other languages have more practical benefits, but Latin is more fun. [Paragraph 2]
    a. It has all of the pleasures of a puzzle, time capsule, and a secret code.
    b. It is like ghost-hunting.
3. Because all of the speakers of Latin are dead, you will never have to learn how to speak it. [Paragraph 3]
    a. There is no pressure to be conversationally fluent or to talk about subjects like your winter break.
4. Latin does not have the vocabulary for discussing some modern subjects (like your winter break), but it does teach you to talk like a supervillain. [Paragraph 4]
    a. Three examples are stated of talking like a supervillain.
    b. Latin immerses you in the world of war, gods, gladiators, and murderous barbers. [Paragraph 5]
5. To study Latin is to engage with the dead, since all we know of Latin comes from people who lived at the time Pompeii was buried by a volcano. [Paragraph 6]
6. The dead Romans have a way of "getting into your head" with their beautiful, useless words. [Paragraph 8]
    a. As an example, the author translates dialogue from a modern sitcom into Latin.
7. Latin teaches that nothing is permanent, not even you or the author. [Paragraph 8]
8. Studying Latin will change your life. It will live in your memory forever. [Paragraph 9]
9. That means that it is not really a dead language at all. [Paragraph 9]

It is instructive to discuss this outline in detail.

The Thesis. A good outline of an argumentative text generally (but not always) will contain a statement of the author's thesis or a restatement of the thesis in your own words. As you now know after our discussion of introductions, the thesis may or may not be stated in the first paragraph.

If you cannot find the author's statement of a thesis, try this strategy. Stop, step back and think about the text as a whole, and ask yourself:

- what is the point of this text? and
- what is the author trying to prove through reasoning from other statements?

If you can answer these questions, then (with very rare exceptions) you can find a sentence (or group of sentences) in the text where the author states that point, his thesis.

If you still cannot find the author's thesis, then stop, think about the text as a whole, and ask yourself:

- is the author really trying to prove some point? and
- am I really reading an argumentative text?

Of course, if you are not reading an argumentative text, but rather one of the other types of nonfiction works we discussed in chapter 4, you will not find a thesis no matter how long you look for it.

In this piece, what is the author's thesis? You reasonably might have more than one answer to that question.

Because a thesis is often found at or near the beginning of an argumentative text, the first sentence of this piece—"If you possibly can get away with it, you should study Latin"—is an obvious candidate for the thesis. It is a bit odd for a thesis to be stated as a conditional statement (*i.e.*, an "if X, then Y" statement). So, ask yourself, what does the antecedent (the "if X" part) of this conditional statement mean?

It is reasonable to read it as meaning, "unless there are insurmountable obstacles" you should study Latin, or "it is really important that you" study Latin. The purpose of the antecedent of the conditional statement, then, is to emphasize the importance of the imperative that is the consequent (the "then Y" part) of the conditional. The thesis, then, can be restated simply as "(most importantly) you should study Latin," or "*study Latin!*" or as a more traditional declarative thesis like, "it is really important that you study Latin."

The author's use of the imperative in the title, and its rephrasing in the first sentence ("you should study Latin"), signals to the reader at the beginning that this is a practical, action-guiding text and is not a mere theoretical discussion of the benefits of learning Latin. In terms we used in the ice cream example in chapter 1 and our discussion of argument types in chapter 4, this is a practical argument, an argument whose conclusion tells someone to do something. The thesis does not expressly state a fact or opinion that the author is trying to prove. Rather, the author is directing you, the reader, to do something—"study Latin." In many articles in the mass media, you will see this sort of use of imperative sentences to give action-guiding direction.

Alternatively, you may read part of the first sentence of the last paragraph—"studying Latin will change your life"—as the thesis. That is not an unreasonable reading of the text. Yet if you do read this as the thesis, what does that commit you to with respect to the nature of the argument in this text? This statement is not action-guiding. It does not tell you or anyone else to do something or what they ought to do. So, if you take it as the thesis of the argument, the conclusion, then you read the text as making a theoretical argument. That reading may be plausible, with some rephrasing of certain sentences. That reading is, however, not easy to square with the expressly stated, action-guiding imperative "study Latin" in the title and the equivalent "you should study Latin" in the first sentence.

Suppose you read the last sentence of the article as stating the thesis. Would that change your outline? Would you place the last sentence at the beginning of your outline, rather than at the end? No. *You generally want to outline a text in the order in which the author has written it.*

This will show you the relations of the ideas in the order that the author has communicated them to you, the audience. That tends to reveal nuances in the argument or other parts of the text that you might otherwise overlook if you were simply looking for the thesis and premises supporting the thesis. It also tends to reveal both the strengths and weaknesses in the argument and highlights passages that may be part of the text but not strictly speaking relevant to the argument. In other words, the author has adopted the structure of the text that she has to communicate some meaning to you that another structure, or a mere recitation of her argument, would not.

To put this lesson slightly differently, *the order of the points of your outline may or may not be precisely the same as the conclusion and premises of an author's argument*. It all depends on (a) what else the author has included in her text that is not strictly relevant to proving her thesis and (b) what the author has omitted from her argument because she assumes you will agree with some unstated point or otherwise believes it need not be stated. We will discuss this point further in the section that follows and elsewhere in this book.

The Structure of the Text. Recall that the structure of a text gives the text meaning. This essay illustrates this lesson in several ways.

Perhaps the first thing you noticed about the outline above is that it does not progress simply in a series of numbered points, 1, 2, 3, 4, and so on. There are numbered points and then subpoints (a., b.) within some of those. What is the difference between an outline that simply has numbers 1, 2, 3, 4, all at the same level of indentation and the one presented here? What does the outline above tell you that you would not get simply by numbering each point 1, 2, 3, 4, or A, B, C, etc.?

Most importantly, look at the relation of the points and subpoints in numbers 2, 3, 4, and 6 of this outline. Notice how the numbered statements are *general* and the subpoints are *particular* statements that are offered to support the general statements or to illustrate them more vividly. Being able to distinguish a general proposition from the specific evidence or other support offered for it is critical in outlining and in reading for understanding. If that is not clear to you, you may want to go back to the article and work through the paragraphs in question with this outline as a guide.

Many argumentative texts make general statements and then offer particular statements in support of the general statements. Knowing this and being able to recognize such general-to-particular reasoning is critical for your understanding of how an argument's premises are connected to each other and to the evidence offered to support them and to give them more concrete meaning. If you were to outline this text simply by putting all of the points of your outline in a simple numerical order—1, 2, 3, etc.—your outline would not visually depict the relations of the general to the particular statements.

Similarly, if you were to outline simply by putting all of the points of your outline in a simple numerical order, your outline would not visually depict which statements are intended by the author to be of the same level of generality (e.g., as are points 1–9 in the outline above) or specificity (as are the subpoints, a., b.). Your outline also would not depict that points 1–9 are the main points the author is employing to prove or emphasize her thesis. In short, an outline in simple numerical order tends to obscure rather than reveal the structural features of an argumentative text that give it meaning.

Let's turn now to two specific elements of our outline. Specifically, subpoints 4.a. and 6.a in our outline are:

4.a Three examples are stated of talking like a supervillain.
6.a. As an example, the author translates dialogue from a sitcom into Latin.

Did you notice something different about these two subpoints, relative to the rest of the outline? These subpoints state what the author *did* in the paragraphs cited, rather than summarizing what the author *says* in those paragraphs as do the other points and subpoints. The outline could have summarized what the author said in those paragraphs, and in some cases that may be preferable for a class assignment. But not necessarily.

The examples offered in paragraph 4 and the Latin dialogue in point 6.a. of the outline (paragraph 8 of the text) are very particular. Once you understand that the thesis (paragraph 1 of the article) is illustrated or supported by these examples and this Latin translation, reciting them in detail does not add much to your understanding of the author's meaning. So, if reading for understanding is your goal, handling those two subpoints as our outline does is fine.

If, however, you wanted to focus on the author's examples or her particular Latin translation, because you were writing a paper criticizing them or otherwise questioning them, you probably would want to summarize in subpoints 4.a. and 6.a. of your outline what the author *says* in that part of the text. How you handle these paragraphs depends on your purposes—and that is another example of how reading for understanding is flexible.

The Argument. Having outlined this essay and determined what its thesis is, you are now in a position to state its argument. Notice that to say that you are "in a position" to state the argument of the text is not to say that you are in a good position. This text offers some challenges in determining its argument.

Does the argument really depend on the reader wanting to "talk like a supervillain"? PBS is in large measure an educational television system. The main audience for the *NewsHour* program is adults. So, you might not be surprised to hear (or read) that a commentator on the *NewsHour* is urging its viewers to do something serious like studying Latin. But it is highly unlikely that the PBS management or staff thinks that many of the viewers of the *NewsHour* walk around everyday thinking, "I wish I could talk like a supervillain."

So, why does the title of this article suggest that some meaningful number of these viewers do want to talk like a supervillain? And if that is so important, why does the author wait until the fourth paragraph to provide examples of what "talking like a supervillain" means?

In a word: rhetoric. "Talking like a supervillain" is catchy. It grabs the reader's attention by appealing to feeling or emotions. If you are a young person in middle or high school and a parent passed this text along to you, you might well think, "wow, that's cool," and be enticed into giving Latin a try.

The title of the essay instead could have declared, "study Latin if you want to change your life." But "change your life" has little power to engage the reader's attention, especially if that reader is, say, under 18. You have heard it 1,000 times. "Talk like a supervillain," on the other hand, is novel, slightly offbeat. It engages your curiosity, and so you keep reading. It may even engage your curiosity sufficiently to get you to enroll in a Latin course.

Once you recognize the rhetorical force of this phrase, where does that leave you in analyzing the argument of the text? You are very likely to ask, is that really the sole premise on which the author is going to rest her entire practical argument that the reader (you) should study Latin? Is the argument of this essay really telling the reader to spend hours studying a language no one uses any more just to have the ability to talk like a fictional supervillain? It is hard to see that a serious news outlet like PBS would waste anyone's time with such a frivolous argument.

At this juncture in your thinking, your outline shows itself to be a useful tool. Your outline makes clear that "talking like a supervillain" is only one of the several benefits of studying Latin. And maybe not even the most important one, even if it sounds like the "coolest" one. So, to capture the meaning of the argument, your restatement should not focus narrowly on this one benefit, but rather should reflect a broader statement of the benefits of studying Latin.

To repeat a lesson from chapter 1, your reformulation of the argument can be more general or more detailed. In other words, what constitutes "the argument" is a matter of *some* flexibility; it is a matter of interpretation and not cast in stone. Put that tool in your toolbox.

So, the argument reasonably and very generally could be restated like this:

> If you want to change your life for the better, study Latin. [Paragraph 1 and final paragraph]
> You want to change your life for the better. [Implied premise]
> Therefore, (you ought to) study Latin. [Conclusion]

Note that the first premise does not focus narrowly on "talking like a supervillain." Rather, it summarizes all of the benefits the author proposes with the phrase, "you want to change your life for the better," which is close to the author's language in the final paragraph of the text.

A fuller restatement of the argument reflects the multiple benefits touted by the author expressly:

> If you want to change your life for the better, study Latin. [Paragraph 1 and final paragraph]
> Studying Latin changes your life for the better by: (a) being fun in many ways (e.g., having the pleasure of a puzzle or time capsule) [Paragraph 2], (b) teaching you phrases that evoke supervillains, war, gods, gladiators, and murderous barbers [Paragraphs 4 and 5], (c) teaching you beautiful words and phrases that you will never forget [Paragraphs 4, 5, and 8], and (d) teaching you the lesson, in unexpected ways (like watching a sitcom), that nothing is permanent, not even you. [Paragraph 8]
> You want to change your life for the better in one or more of these ways. [Implied premise]
> Few things, if any, are more important than changing your life for the better. [Paragraph 1, or implied premise]
> Therefore, (you *really ought to*) study Latin [or, it is really important that you study Latin]. [Conclusion]

This more detailed restatement shows that talking like a supervillain is only one of the benefits touted. And, like the essay itself, it places those supervillains in a context of a history of Rome that includes similarly exotic characters and events, like wars, gods, and gladiators, and in a modern cultural context where learning Latin is a way of appreciating the beauty of its words for their own sake and adding meaning to trivial art forms like TV sitcoms.

Note that these two restatements of the argument include one or two premises that are not expressly stated in the article itself. As they appear in the first restatement, it is:

You want to change your life for the better. [Implied premise]

In the second restatement, they are:

You want to change your life for the better in one or more of these ways. [Implied premise]
Few things, if any, are more important than changing your life for the better. [Paragraph 1, or implied premise]

(Whether this second statement is implied or is a restatement of the first clause of paragraph 1 ("if you can possibly get away with it") depends on how one interprets that ambiguous clause.)

Why are these statements included as premises when the author herself did not include them? Recall our discussion of enthymemes in chapter 4. Without these implied premises, the other premises do not alone support the conclusion. In other words, without them, the conclusion does not follow from just the other premises alone. The article is telling the reader to do something, "study Latin." But if the reader is happy with her life as it is and does not want to change it for the better, then she does not have to accept the direction to "study Latin." So, for the conclusion to follow from the stated premises, there must be unstated, implied, premises that show that it does apply to the reader.

As you read in chapter 4, it is common for arguments to imply, but not expressly state, one or more premises that is (are) needed to support the conclusion that the author intends to prove with her expressly stated premises. As an example of such an enthymatic argument, this essay is instructive. Put this tool in your reading toolbox: *you should not expect a completely articulated argument, with each necessary premise expressly stated, in most nonacademic texts, especially texts designed for a mass audience.* Here, we do not have such a fully articulated argument because certain premises are implied and not expressly stated.

AN OPINION PIECE ON VOTING RIGHTS

In the late 1960s, in the midst of the Vietnam War and cultural upheaval in this country, one of the hot public debates was whether the voting age for federal elections should be lowered from twenty-one years old to eighteen. In 1971, the debate ended when the U.S. Constitution was amended to lower the voting age to eighteen. That debate was part of our long history of debate over who should be allowed to participate in our democratic institutions through the ballot box. Of course, after the Civil War, the federal franchise was extended to African American men (through the Fifteenth Amendment), and in 1920 it was extended to women. In 2018, Representative Ayanna Pressley of Massachusetts introduced legislation in the House of Representatives to extend the franchise to people as young as sixteen years old.

Read the article, "Ayanna Pressley Is Right: 16-Year-Olds Deserve the Right to Vote," attached at Appendix B.[3] This article appeared in *Newsweek* online and is fairly typical of the sorts of argumentative pieces you will find in the mass media. After you have read it, do an outline of the article, and only when you have done that, come back and read the following analysis.

You have done your outline. Because you are new to outlining, let's take a look at this model outline and then you can compare the two.

1. For our democracy to function as it should, we need to encourage more Americans from diverse backgrounds (racial, socioeconomic, age-related) to vote. [Paragraph 1]
2. Recently, much has been made of the fragility of American democracy. [Paragraph 3]
    a. Commentators of all political persuasions complain about low voter turnout and that large segments of American public are apathetic, uninformed, or illegitimate. [Paragraph 3]
3. Few organizations or legislators have proposed the bold solutions needed to increase the representativeness of our electorate. [Paragraph 4]
4. A compelling and democratic idea has been offered by Ayanna Pressley to lower the federal voting age to sixteen. [Paragraph 5]
    a. It was not well received in House of Representatives. [Paragraph 5]
    b. The House of Representatives said that sixteen-year-olds cannot reasonably contribute to the electoral process. [Paragraph 5]
    c. "We" say that sixteen-year-olds lack maturity and experience to make informed voting decisions and will just vote as their parents do. [Paragraph 7]

5. We do not have a good reason to deny the vote to sixteen-year-olds. To the contrary, evidence suggests that enfranchising sixteen-year-olds is good for them and for our democracy. [Paragraph 8]
   a. Greta Thunberg and students from Parkland High School are examples of adolescents who exhibit independent thought, deep understanding, clear convictions, maturity, and poise. Also, they are well informed and engaged. [Paragraph 9]
   b. The notion that they are ill informed and inexperienced echoes reasons given for not allowing women and African Americans to vote. [Paragraph 10]
   c. Sixteen-year-olds are taxpayers. [Paragraph 10]
   d. Politicians today are making decisions affecting sixteen-year-olds.
   e. Sixteen-year-olds will be living with the consequences of those decisions for a lot longer than most current voters. [Paragraph 10]
   f. A scientific study from National Academies of Science, Engineering, and Medicine shows that adolescents have many traits which are essential to participation in the electoral process, including an increased capacity for complex reasoning, strategic problem solving, and others. [Paragraph 11]
   g. The same research shows that there is no better way to promote sustained civic engagement than to nurture voting in teenagers and make it part of their identity formation. Habits formed in these teenage years can be long lasting. [Paragraph 12]
   h. Takoma Park, Maryland, allowed sixteen- and seventeen-year-olds to vote in local elections.
      - Six years of evidence shows these voters vote at nearly double the rate of voters 18-years-old and over. [Paragraph 14]
6. The notion that adolescents are incapable of the sober judgment needed to vote is a misguided prejudice against young people. It is not a basis for denying adolescents a say in our democracy. [Paragraph 15]
7. It is time to enfranchise sixteen-year-olds. [Paragraph 16]

You may find that your outline of this essay differs from this one. Those differences, if any, are not a cause for concern. This outline is not "right" and yours "wrong," or vice versa. Recall this maxim from chapter 3—there is no one authoritative reading of a text.

When you encounter differences in the interpretation of a text (say, the differences between your interpretation and a friend's), what do you do? *Treat those differences as an opportunity for further inquiry as to which reading more closely captures the author's meaning.* Maybe both readings could benefit from closer scrutiny of the text. Maybe one reading just missed something the other reading did not. Maybe the text is thoroughly ambiguous at one or more critical junctures. Only when you have chased down each of these possibilities can you say with confidence that one reading is "better" than the other.

The Thesis. The thesis is stated in the very last sentence of this essay—"It is time to enfranchise 16-year-olds," or, as stated in the title, "16-year-olds deserve the right to vote." Either version of this thesis could be restated as, "The federal government should pass a law that lowers the voting age to 16" or, as an imperative, "Change federal law to extend the right to vote to people as young as 16 years old." When rephrased in this fashion, we see that the author is asserting a practical argument—the federal government should do something.

The Structure of the Text. What does the structure of this text tell us about what the author intends to communicate?

For purposes of analyzing this piece, we begin by asking, what type of introduction does the author, Ms. Deutsch, employ and how is it related to the rest of her text?[4] The first paragraph, which is one sentence long, appears to be stating a problem, namely, our democracy is not functioning as it should. And it appears to be stating a solution to the problem, namely, to encourage greater diversity in our electorate in federal and local elections.

That *seems* straightforward. Yet what does the author mean when she says that our "democracy [is not] function[ing] as it should?" Does it mean that our democracy is not providing everyone with "life, liberty, and the pursuit of happiness," as stated in the *Declaration of Independence*, and it should be doing that? Does it mean that it is failing to give everyone's opinion due consideration in decision-making processes, whatever outcomes that produces? Something else? When you see an ambiguous phrase like "for our democracy to function as it should . . .," especially when it is part of the statement of the problem that the essay is attempting to solve, you will not understand the text unless you figure out what that phrase means. (We discuss ambiguity in more depth in chapter 7.)

Fortunately, the author appears to tell us what she means by this phrase in paragraph 3, when she writes that pundits "complain about notoriously low voter turnout, decrying large segments of the voting public as apathetic, uninformed or even illegitimate." So, apparently her view is that our democracy is not functioning as it should because of low voter turnout and because large segments of the American public are apathetic, uninformed, or illegitimate. And the "bold solution" for that set of problems is to increase the representativeness of our electorate (paragraph 4).

In a nutshell, the first four paragraphs of this opinion piece appear to be intended to articulate a problem for which an expansion of voting rights to include sixteen- and seventeen-year-olds is said to be the solution or part of a solution. This reading appears to be confirmed by the fact that the argument in favor of giving sixteen-year-olds the right to vote begins with paragraph 5.

If that is correct, then why does Deutsch think that the solution to this set of problems (low voter turnout and that large segments of American public are apathetic, uninformed, or illegitimate) is to encourage greater diversity in our electorate in federal and local elections, as opposed to any number of other solutions? Why does she think that her "bold" solution is needed, rather than, say, a more mundane solution like making voter registration easier, giving everyone a paid day off from work to vote, eliminating gerrymandering, limiting the amount of money one person can contribute to a political candidate, and so on? Does her rhetorical use of "bold" add anything to her argument?

You will recall that a major premise of this book is that understanding an argumentative text involves understanding both the argument made and how the parts of the text that are not strictly part of the argument illuminate or obscure the meaning of the argument. In reading this essay, that means analyzing the relationship between the way Deutsch has framed her problem in the first four paragraphs, on the one hand, and her solution to it, on the other hand. Assume she has a very good practical argument for lowering the voting age. Is that the right solution for the problem (or problems) that large segments of American public are apathetic, uninformed, or illegitimate? Is she offering a single solution to a set of problems for which there is no single solution?

In short, *when an argumentative text begins by stating a problem, understanding the meaning of the text includes understanding as precisely as possible what the author thinks that problem is, and is not, and whether the author's argument provides a solution to it or misses the mark.* That's an important tool for your toolbox.

One further note on the structure of this text. Look at number 5 in the outline above. The points a. through h. under number 5 are offered to support the assertions made in number 5. Examine these points carefully. Do they state one or several types of reasons in support of number 5? How are subpoints a. through h. related, if they are?

These subpoints express three different kinds of reasons. First, subpoints 5.a, b., f., and g. speak to the intellectual and emotional capacities of adolescents, and state that these are sufficiently developed that adolescents should be allowed to vote. Second, subpoints 5.c., d., and e. in our outline reflect a different idea—that those who will feel the consequences of a law (e.g., as taxpayers) should be able to participate in the process by which the law is enacted or formulated. Third, subpoint 5.h and its subpoint refer to evidence that when sixteen- and seventeen-year-olds are allowed to vote, a higher percentage of them vote than do other age-related voting groups.

So, what does the author communicate when she presents these three types of reasons in the manner she does? From a purely logical point of view, one would think that her first type of reasons (subpoints 5.a., b., f., and g.) would be all grouped together and not interrupted by her second type of reasons (points 5.c., d., and e.). Does her presentation of this second set of subpoints suggest that she has less confidence in these than in her first set (subpoints 5.a., b., f., and g.), so she buries them in the middle of these other subpoints? Would her argument be more powerful if she began with her second type of reasons and made her first type dependent on that?

In other words, would her argument be more powerful if she proceeded in this fashion: "We fought our Revolutionary War to defeat taxation without representation and to uphold the belief that a government is legitimate only if there is consent of the governed; it is in the Declaration of Independence. (That is essentially her second type of reason, although stated more generally.) So, any person who has the intellectual and emotional capabilities to cast an informed vote should be allowed to do so. People as young as sixteen years old have those capabilities. (That is her first type of reason.)"

The tool for your toolbox is: *It is common to find argumentative texts in which the author downplays, or does not include at all, reasons that could strengthen (or weaken) the thesis that the author is attempting to prove. Analyzing the types of reasons offered for a conclusion and the manner in which they are presented provides insights into the author's meaning and the ways her argument may be reformulated to add support for (or to undermine) her thesis.*

Because the structure of the rest of this essay is a fairly clear statement of the author's argument, it is not necessary to walk through it in detail here. It will be more productive to examine that argument.

The Argument. From your outline, you should be able to take the major points of the author's essay and restate them into her argument, omitting the points that are not part of her argument. Give it a try. Do a very general and then a more detailed reconstruction of her argument. If you are having trouble getting started, you already know what her thesis is, so you can make that the conclusion of the argument, and then the other points would precede that.

You are back. You have restated her argument. Compare your general restatement with this one:

Our democracy is not functioning as it should. [Premise]
To make it function as it should, we need to increase representativeness of our electorate. [Premise]
We can increase the representativeness of our electorate by encouraging more Americans from diverse backgrounds (racial, socioeconomic, age-related) to vote. [Premise]

Lowering the federal voting age to sixteen would increase the representation of an age-related group. [Premise]
Therefore, it is time to (we should) enfranchise sixteen-year-olds. [Conclusion]

A more detailed restatement of the argument would take account of the evidence the author employs to support certain of her premises. For your ease of reference, the bullets highlight the statements of her evidence.

Our democracy is not functioning as it should. [Premise]
- Commentators of all political persuasions complain about low voter turnout and that large segments of American public are apathetic, uninformed, or illegitimate. [Subpremise]

To make it function as it should, we need to increase representativeness of our electorate. [Premise]
We can increase the representativeness of our electorate by encouraging more Americans from diverse backgrounds (racial, socioeconomic, age-related) to vote. [Premise]
Lowering the federal voting age to sixteen would increase the representativeness of our electorate. [Premise]
We do not have a good reason to deny the vote to sixteen-year-olds. [Premise]
To the contrary, evidence suggests enfranchising sixteen-year-olds is good for them and for our democracy. [Premise]
- Greta Thunberg and students from Parkland High School are examples of independent thought, deep understanding, clear convictions, maturity, and poise. Also, they are well informed and engaged. [Subpremise]
- Sixteen-year-olds are taxpayers. [Subpremise]
- Politicians today are making decisions affecting sixteen-year-olds. [Subpremise]
- Sixteen-year-olds will be living with the consequences of those decisions for a lot longer than most current voters. [Subpremise]
- A scientific study from the National Academies of Science, Engineering, and Medicine shows that adolescents have many traits which are essential to participation in the electoral process, including an increased capacity for complex reasoning, strategic problem solving, and others. [Subpremise]
- The same research shows no better way to promote sustained civic engagement that to nurture it in teens and make it part of identity formation. Habits formed in these years can be long lasting. [Subpremise]

- Takoma Park, Maryland, allowed sixteen- and seventeen-year-olds to vote. Six years of evidence shows that when sixteen- and seventeen-year-olds are allowed to vote, they do so at nearly double the rate of voters eighteen and over. [Subpremise]

The notion that adolescents lack the intelligence and developmental traits we require of others to vote is a misguided prejudice. [Premise]
- The notion that sixteen- and seventeen-year-olds are ill informed and inexperienced reprises the reasons given for not allowing women and African Americans to vote. [Subpremise]

Therefore, it is time to (we ought to) enfranchise sixteen-year-olds. [Conclusion]

Having presented a detailed statement of the argument, let's focus on the next-to-the-last premise and three of the subpremises offered to support it:

Evidence suggests enfranchising sixteen-year-olds is good for them and for our democracy. [Premise]
- Sixteen-year-olds are taxpayers. [Subpremise]
- Politicians today are making decisions affecting sixteen-year-olds. [Subpremise]
- Sixteen-year-olds will be living with the consequences of those decisions for a lot longer than most current voters. [Subpremise]

Do these three subpremises support the premise they are offered to support? What does the author mean when she says that "enfranchising 16-year-olds is good for them?" In what way is it "good for them?" What if sixteen-year-olds generally vote for the "worst" candidates with the "worst" policies? What assumptions are built into this statement by the author, and in the related claim that "enfranchising 16-year-olds is good for . . . our democracy?" What sort of evidence, beyond the evidence she has already offered, would she need to support these assumptions?

This essay gives us a lot to think about. Outlining the essay, examining its statement of the problem it purports to solve, and restating its argument reveal both its strengths and limitations. With your greater understanding of this text and its argument, you are now in a better position to assess its merits.

SUMMARIES: THE BIG PICTURE IN A NUTSHELL

Think about your favorite movie. Suppose your friend has not seen it and is wondering whether he should hop on a streaming service to watch it. He asks you, "What is it about?"

The question is not, "Is it any good?" He is not asking you for a literary or artistic judgment about the movie. His question also is not, "Should I watch it?" He is not asking for your opinion whether it is worth his time to watch this movie or whether he would find it enjoyable. He wants to know whether you can summarize its essential elements in a few sentences. So, try it. Before you go any further, pick your favorite movie and write a summary in a short paragraph.

Compare your summary with the summaries you can find online about the same movie. What do those summaries have that yours lacks, and vice versa?

Typically, if a friend asks you to summarize a movie so that he can decide whether to watch it (or if he is just curious as to what it is about), he will want to know what kind of movie it is (fantasy, science fiction, comedy, romance, biography, etc.), who the principal characters are, a general statement of the plot (the story the movie is trying to tell), who the principal actors are, and, if he is really into movies, who directed it. Does your summary have at least these elements?

We use a summary of an argumentative text to test or communicate our understanding of the meaning of a text. For a reader who is trying to understand an argumentative text, a summary is a useful way of stepping back and asking: what is the point of the text? what do I know about the text? Because argumentative texts generally do not have a plot (or narrative structure) and generally do not have leading characters, a summary of an argumentative text will differ in meaningful respects from your summary of a movie.[5]

For any argumentative text, once you have outlined it, and refined the outline as necessary, you then will be in a position to step back and summarize the text in a few sentences or paragraphs. If you think of the outline as the trees as you are hiking through the woods, your summary is the view of the forest from the top of the mountain at the end of your hike. It is the big picture, but compressed into a nutshell.

The "big picture"—it is a nice metaphor but it does not give you much guidance. So, here is what you need to know. Generally, your summary should summarize your outline. At a minimum, it should state:

1. the name of the author,
2. the title of the work you are summarizing,
3. the author's thesis (what is the point the author is trying to prove?),
4. the main points he made in attempting to prove the thesis, and
5. a mention of the evidence or *types* of evidence he employs.

A few caveats and comments are in order.

First, on elements (1) and (2), if you are summarizing just a small part of an entire book or article and the reader already knows which work you are summarizing, you may not need to include the author's name and the title of the text.

Second, when setting forth the author's thesis (element [3]), it often is helpful to state the problem or issue the author is attempting to address. For example, "The author's analysis of social justice in urban America in the early twenty-first-century attempts to provide a contemporary answer to the classical question, 'what is justice?' His answer to that question is, [then state his thesis]" or, "The author is attempting to predict the social impacts of the widespread use of artificial intelligence. He argues, [state his thesis]."

Third, on element (5), the author may be relying on, for example, statistical data of a population, passages from the Bible, his interpretation of historical events, or the analysis of a concept (e.g., courage or beauty). Noting the evidence or the type of evidence he employs is suggestive (and only suggestive) of how successful the author is in proving his thesis; his evidence at least has to be in the right ballpark. You would not be surprised to find a lot of jokes used as evidence in an essay on the nature of comedy, but if those same jokes were used as the only evidence in an essay on human rights or urban poverty, the author would have to do some work to explain that incongruity.

Fourth, a summary does not include your commentary on the work. For example, in this sentence, "he tried to prove that Warren G. Harding was the best president of the twentieth century, *but the author failed miserably*," the italicized words state unnecessary commentary. Your commentary is not essential to your summary because the summary reflects your understanding of the thesis the author is trying to prove and how he attempts to prove it. Whether you think the author's thesis is right or wrong, or whether his proof of that point is strong or weak, is *not* essential to whether you understand the work and can state that understanding succinctly.

As you learned in chapter 3, in reading for understanding, *you need to put your opinions (and ego) on hold and focus on what another person—the author—is saying*. Focusing on what *you* say, or think, or feel about what he is saying is to miss the point of trying to understand *his text*.

Putting your opinions and ego on hold is contrary to so much of our culture today that it may actually seem odd to you, or just wrong. If you take the talking and shouting heads on CNN, Fox, or MSNBC to be the gold standard of intellectual exchange, you may well think that "putting your opinions and ego on hold" is incomprehensible or wrongheaded. The only meaningful response to this is: put the tools in this book to serious, extended, and focused use, and then see if you still have the same opinion.

One final thought on summaries. Is your summary of a text the same summary you would use in a paper you are writing about that text? It depends. In writing a paper, you may want to stress certain parts of the author's argument and pay less attention to other parts. You might do this, for example, if you are writing a paper that takes issue with only one of the points the author made in her argument. That is acceptable, as long as your summary does not distort the work you are writing about. Setting up and knocking down a "straw man" or "straw woman" is a sign of intellectual weakness, not strength. In short, the purpose of your summary in your paper will dictate the contents of that summary, what you include and exclude and the stress you put on what you include.

WHAT IS THE POINT?

We have covered a lot of detailed ground in this chapter, and so it is helpful to step back and take a broader perspective on outlining and summarizing. Let's start with what you do when your outline or summary of a text differs from that of another reader or when your summary differs from one offered by the author.

Those sorts of differences in interpretation are not cause for despair. They *are* an occasion for further inquiry. Ask yourself—why are they different? If your summary of an essay differs from the author's, is it because you are reading the essay one hundred years after it was written and you are able to compare it with a lot of later texts that have addressed the same problem and that the author never read? Is it because you do not share the author's political or cultural convictions? Have you simply missed something basic or essential in the work and do not really have a good grasp of what the author is trying to communicate? Is it because you have not read the text closely enough, have not grasped the details sufficiently?

Understanding the reasons for different interpretations of a text is a crucial element in understanding what the text can reasonably be interpreted to mean. Those differences are *starting points* for greater *understanding*—improved understanding of a subject matter you never studied before, of a point of view you had not considered before or one that you had considered before and rejected, of how your opinions are without a reasonable foundation or are even better grounded than you had known, of what it means to be *a person* in this society, this world, this time. And not to be lost in this discussion, with better understanding comes increased confidence and a greater ability for you to engage with the world in more productive and meaningful ways. Greater understanding is empowering.

After reading this chapter and studying the examples in detail, you may be thinking: "Holy mackerel! If I do what he's talking about here for everything I have to read, it will take me forever. I'll flunk all of my courses." Many students have known this thought all too well. It is a sinking feeling. Drowning in work.

One effect of outlining, summarizing, taking notes, writing comments in the margins, and underlining is to slow you down while reading. Each of these causes you to read a text more carefully and more thoughtfully. They cause you to pay attention to what is in the text and what is not there, to grasp the important details and ignore the unimportant ones, to concentrate on what the author intends to communicate to you.

The good news is that as you get better at reading argumentative texts, you will be able to better understand them without employing one or more of these tools. A master chef may have to read the recipe for a dish the first time he is making it, but not when he is making it the hundredth time. You too will know more about how to read for understanding the more you practice the basics, to the point where you can put aside these tools when you get to the place where they are impeding your progress. You *will* get there, with practice.

NOTES

1. "Op-ed" is shorthand for opposite the editorial page. It refers to opinion pieces in newspapers that generally are found on the page immediately after the page (on the opposite page) that contains the editorials published by the newspaper's editorial board.

2. Also available at, Opinion: Study Latin if you want to talk like a supervillain | PBS NewsHour.

3. Also available at newsweek.com/ayanna-pressley-right-16-year-olds-deserve-right-vote-opinion-1469043.

4. You could, of course, begin by analyzing how your outline graphically depicts how particular points are used to support more general statements or how the numbered statements in the outline are all of the same level of generality. The type of introduction Deutsch uses suggests a different approach may be more illuminating. There is no single "right" strategy to begin your analysis of every text.

5. "Generally" in this sentence indicates that histories may be an exception to this statement. Historical accounts sometimes are written with a narrative structure, even while they make an argument about an historical event or person. Biographies are a good example of such "mixed" texts.

Chapter 7

Ambiguity and Nonliteral Uses of Language

Reading woke me up. It took me from a world of harsh limits into expanded possibility.—Mark Edmundson, *Why Read?* p. 1 (New York: Bloomsbury 2004)

Once you understand the kind of introduction the author has used in a text (chapter 5), and after you have done an outline and summary (chapter 6), you still may be far from understanding a text. Introductions, outlines, and summaries all deal with the big picture, the view from 20,000 feet.

To understand a text, you also need to know what it looks like at ground level. You need to understand its particulars. These particulars include: an author's use of an ambiguous word, phrase, sentence, or paragraph; the difference between factual and normative statements; what the author is doing when she uses words that do not mean what they literally say (irony); how an author may appeal to emotions, feeling, or shared values to persuade her readers (rhetoric); and how an author's conclusion really does, or does not, follow from her premises (the logical connections between terms).

Understanding many texts requires squeezing the author's intended meaning out of one sentence, one phrase in a sentence, or one word. That is especially important when the word, phrase, or sentence is vague or may have more than one meaning. Recall that in our analysis of the essay on lowering the voting age (chapter 6) we began by asking what the author meant by the phrase, "for our democracy to function as it should." In the first section of this chapter, we drill down deeper on ambiguous words, phrases, and sentences. In the next section we discuss how to understand three types of nonliteral uses of language that are keys to understanding the particulars of a text.

Chapter 7

TWO KINDS OF AMBIGUITY

For our purposes, a word, phrase, sentence, or group of sentences is ambiguous when it (or they) can be *reasonably* interpreted in more than one way. "The chicken is ready to eat" is ambiguous (and humorous) because it may mean either that the chicken is near his food and ready to eat it or that the chicken is cooked and is now ready to be eaten. "Quadruplicity stardust mooga" is not ambiguous because it has no reasonable interpretation. It is nonsense.

Ambiguity is pervasive. Sometimes the author strives for clarity and yet the text is ambiguous. In other cases, an author may intend a term or sentence to be ambiguous. Many jokes turn on the ambiguity of a word or sentence, so we will start with some humorous examples.

1. It's a small world, but I wouldn't want to paint it. (Steven Wright)
2. A lawyer walks into a restaurant with his alligator. He asks the waitperson, "Do you serve lawyers?"
   The waitperson responds, "Of course."
   The lawyer says, "Great. I'll have a hamburger and my alligator will have a lawyer." (Common lawyer joke)
3. Bert: I know a man with a wooden leg named Smith.
   Uncle Albert: What was the name of his other leg? (from the movie *Mary Poppins*)
4. One morning I shot an elephant in my pajamas. How he got into my pajamas I'll never know. (Groucho Marx)

In the first two examples, the ambiguity arises out of the multiple meanings of a common phrase, a figure of speech. (Ambiguity that arises out of a word or phrase is called semantic ambiguity. You do not need to memorize the term, just know how to recognize it when you encounter it.) "It's a small world" can refer to the actual size of the earth or figuratively refer to the closeness of social connections in a community. It usually refers to the latter, and the humor is that the speaker takes it to mean the former. In the second example, "do you serve X" can refer to what the restaurant has on its menu ("do you serve herbal tea?") or to a person or class of persons who want service ("do you serve people with no shoes or shirts?"). The joke identifies the customer as a lawyer, and so when he asks, "do you serve lawyers?" we expect him to be using the phrase in the second sense, while his instructions to the waitperson give it its first meaning.

In the final two examples, the ambiguity arises out of the structure of the sentence itself, or group of sentences, and not any one word or phrase. (This is sometimes referred to as syntactic ambiguity. Again, you do not need to memorize the term, just know how to recognize it when you encounter it.) By placing "named Smith" at the end of the sentence in the third example, it is unclear whether that phrase refers to the man (which it would normally do) or his wooden leg (which it might do because of the proximity of "wooden leg" to "named Smith"). Similarly, in the fourth example, "in my pajamas" is located next to "an elephant," and so may refer to that animal, rather than to the speaker ("I shot") which normally would be the person wearing pajamas.

Of course, the ambiguity of a word, phrase, or sentence (semantic ambiguity, which is independent of the structure of the sentence) does not always lend itself to humor. Such ambiguity is commonly found when a term, phrase, or sentence states or implies a broad moral, political, or aesthetic judgment. To consider just one example, before you read any further, take a moment and write down your best definition of "freedom."

How does it compare to these definitions?

- "Freedom" is the absence of constraints. (A common definition in philosophical works.)
- "Freedom's just another word for nothing left to lose." (Kris Kristofferson, "Me and Bobby McGee," a pop song)
- Freedom is having a safe ride home. Don't drink and drive. (A sign on an interstate highway in Indiana, July 4, 2019)

It is unlikely that your definition is exactly the same as any of these. Freedom is a broad concept, and when used in an argumentative philosophical work (or a pop song or a highway sign), it is capable of having many reasonable meanings.

Similarly, the ambiguity that arises from the structure of a sentence or group of sentences (syntactic ambiguity) does not depend on the placement of a phrase at the end of a sentence and, of course, is not always humorous.

"Racing cars can be dangerous" is ambiguous and not funny. It can reasonably mean that (a) racing cars can be dangerous for the drivers who are driving those cars or (b) having cars racing around (anywhere) can create a dangerous condition for pedestrians, spectators, and so on.

Or, for one final example, consider: "The doctor said on Wednesday he'd be playing golf." Does that mean that (a) on Wednesday the doctor said "I'll be playing golf [at some future time]" or (b) the doctor said, at some point in time, that he would be playing golf on Wednesday? Either interpretation is reasonable given the structure of the sentence, and so it is ambiguous.

You get the idea. We need not say more here about ambiguity.

Chapter 7

NONLITERAL USES OF LANGUAGE

It would be a reader's paradise if ambiguous terms, phrases, and sentences were the only impediments to understanding an author's meaning. But you know that life is never *that* easy.

So, in this section we will discuss three kinds of nonliteral uses of language that may make it easier or more difficult for you to understand an author's meaning. First, we will look at normative statements, and specifically the distinction between factual statements and normative statements. Second, we will examine ironic statements. And, finally, we will return to rhetoric. Because such usages are common, familiarity with them is often essential to understanding what an author is trying to communicate and assessing how well founded his views are.

What do these types of statement have in common? If our minds were very simple, we would only use language very literally to refer to facts in the world. For example, "Some dogs weigh more than 100 pounds" and "granite is a nonporous rock" are literal, factual statements. "My gorilla is in the living room watching TV" literally means that it is a fact about the world that my gorilla is in the living room watching TV. If you ask a stranger how to get to the movie theater, he may say, "it's two blocks south of here and three blocks west." That is a very literal, fact-based used of language. If he is correct, then the movie theater is where he said it is.

In our world, however, we often use language not literally to refer to facts, but rather to express certain rules or values, to say something just the opposite of the literal meaning of the words, or to persuade through appeals to emotions or sentiments or the character of the speaker. This section discusses these three types of nonfactual and nonliteral uses of language.

Normative Statements: Values Are Not Facts

Let's start this discussion with what you already know—a *factual* statement purports to tell you something about the world that is true and that can be proven true through one of your senses (sight, smell, etc.) or through scientific methods and tools. For example, "all humans are mortal," "roses smell different than carnations," and "I have a headache" are all factual statements.

In contrast, *normative* statements are statements that imply a rule, a norm, or a value. You will often see ethical, moral, practical, legal, or aesthetic views or opinions referred to as normative statements. You may also hear such statements referred to as "value judgments" because they express or imply some value, for example, what it is good or right or just to do, that a painting is beautiful, or the like. Here are a few simple examples of normative statements:

- "a punishment ought to fit the crime"
- "it is wrong to lie"
- "if you want to be (if you value being) a good parent, then you should practice patience"
- "Van Gogh's *Starry Night* is the most beautiful painting ever painted"

Normative statements often (but not always) contain moral terms like "right," "wrong," "duty," "good," evil," or judgments as to beauty or its absence ("the sunset was beautiful last night," "that's an ugly dog"), or judgments as to quality or lack of quality ("Jimi Hendrix was the best guitarist ever," "that was a terrible movie"). To clarify a bit, "because the earth spins counterclockwise, the sun *must* rise in the east" is not a normative statement. Here, "must" simply refers to a physical necessity and does not express a value or rule of action. But, "you *must* stop smoking" is a normative statement, because "must" means "absolutely should" or "necessarily ought" (if you value a longer life or good health).

The smoking example illustrates that while many uses of "ought" or "should" imply a moral, legal, or aesthetic value, not all of them do. These terms may instead be used to express the view that some action is prudent to do because you value something else that is prudent or practical (and not moral, legal, or aesthetic). "You ought to brush your teeth three times a day" typically means something like, "it is prudent to brush your teeth three times a day because you do not want your teeth to fall out (or, you do not value your teeth falling out)." "You should pay your taxes" may mean something like, "if you want to avoid (do not value) paying a large fine, then it is prudent to pay your taxes." In other words, if you value some practical end or goal (like having good oral hygiene or avoiding a big fine), then do action X.

We briefly touched on prudential normative statements already, in chapters 1 and 4 when we discussed action-guiding statements. In our ice cream example, "you should eat some ice cream" is a conclusion of an argument one of whose premises is "you want to cool off," which is equivalent to, "you value cooling off" or "you think cooling off is good."

Recall the essay "Study Latin if you want to talk like a supervillain," which we discussed in chapter 6. Suppose that sentence was rewritten like this:

If you want to talk like a supervillain, study Latin.

This is easily rephrased as:

If you want to talk like a supervillain, you ought to study Latin.

In other words:

If you value talking like a supervillain, then you ought to (or should) study Latin.

These sorts of uses of "ought" and "should" are normative statements because they embody prudential (or practical) values or norms (rather than moral, legal, aesthetic, or qualitative ones). Think of it this way—there are some things we just want or value for reasons wholly independent of morality, the law, aesthetic considerations, or general qualitative considerations. Those generally are prudential values. Wanting to talk like a supervillain or wanting to be healthy are prudential, as is thinking it would be good to eat that ice cream cone. We generally value something prudentially when it makes us happy, allows us to avoid pain, or allows us to feel pleasure. A whole lot more could be said about prudential values and the normative statements that express them, but you get the general idea.

This distinction between factual statements and normative statements is especially important in understanding many texts you will be reading (or speeches or lectures you may hear) because these types of sentences seem to refer to two different aspects of reality—facts and values (or norms). And yet they are often thrown together in an argument as if the logical connections between them were obvious or self-evident. Specifically, for example, if you read anything in current political debates, it is very common to find the author reciting a litany of facts and drawing a normative conclusion from them.

So, you may be asking, what is wrong with that? Well, as the Scottish philosopher David Hume (1711–1786) observed, a factual statement *alone* does not imply, or allow one to draw a conclusion to, a specific normative statement. There is no rule of logic or argument that allows us to draw a normative conclusion (about rights and duties, beauty, and so on) solely from one or more factual statements. So, every time an author or speaker piles up a bunch of facts and draws a normative conclusion from them alone, there is something "fishy" going on.

Usually what is "fishy" is that the author is appealing to an unstated norm or value. If she is making an argument, it is an enthymeme. There is nothing wrong with that *as a practical matter.* Speakers and authors routinely do not articulate every statement needed to support their conclusion; they rightly assume we can fill in the gaps. The important point for you as a reader is to recognize that an author's thesis may follow from her expressly stated premises only if one or more unstated normative statements are also part of her argument. To understand the author's meaning and what she is asking you to commit to, you need to understand the implicit norms or value judgments that inform her position.

To take a simple example, suppose it is a fact that one million children starve to death each year in Asia. What normative conclusion follows (with necessity or probability) from that fact? Consider these possibilities, all of which are normative (they state what someone should do in these circumstances, based on some rule or value).

- Men and women in Asia should have fewer children.
- Affluent citizens of the industrialized world ought to feed these children.
- You have a duty to give money to an international aid organization like Save the Children.
- The governments of the countries in which these children reside are violating their rights by allowing them to starve.

None of these follows from the factual premise (one million children starve to death each year in Asia) alone, and yet all are related to it in some fashion. Even if you were to add a lot more facts to the discussion, no normative conclusion *necessarily* or *probably* follows *just* from those facts. Try it. (That is in large part why political debates are never just about the facts.)

So, when you read an essay or book with normative statements about what you, someone else, or a government should do or not do, or ought to do or not do, or what rights or duties a person or group has, you need to ask yourself, what is the basis for those normative statements if it is not some set of facts alone? How does the author know that this is what you or your government should do?

To make sure we do not lose the forest for the trees, the tool to put in your reading toolbox is: *because facts alone cannot support a normative conclusion, when an author argues for a normative conclusion ask whether the author's argument includes an express or implied normative premise, which, in addition to its expressly stated factual premises, would support the normative conclusion. If it does, then once you have determined what that normative premise is, you will better understand what normative commitments the author is making and asking you to accept in arguing for his conclusion.*

A couple of examples will help flesh out this lesson.

Example 1. Consider this simple argument made by the author, playwright, and actor Wallace Shawn,[1] which is edited slightly from the original.

> Punishment and revenge are unjust because there's absolutely no way to determine that the person being punished, or the person against whom revenge is taken, was capable of behaving differently from the way they behaved.[2]

Now, what is the argument Shawn is making? What is the premise (or premises) of the argument? There is only one premise stated, and that is everything that comes after the word "because":

> There's absolutely no way to determine that the person being punished, or the person against whom revenge is taken, was capable of behaving differently from the way they behaved.

And from this sole premise, Shawn concludes:

> [Therefore], punishment and revenge are unjust.

(Note that Shawn has stated his conclusion first and his premise after that.) This conclusion is a normative statement because it expresses a moral or ethical conclusion (acts of punishment and revenge are unjust). So, does this conclusion necessarily or probably follow from the premise? A moment's reflection shows that it does not.

First, can you think of any counterarguments to Shawn's argument? How about this one? Suppose we do not prove that a murderer really was not capable of acting differently than he did. Suppose we simply accept that he had no choice or free will in committing the murder. Does that mean it would be unjust to (that we *should not*) punish him by locking him up in jail or in a mental institution?

If you said a tiger was not capable of acting other than it did when it ate a person, that would seem to be a strong argument for keeping the tiger locked up, not a reason for saying "it's unjust to lock it up." Otherwise, it always will be a deadly threat to the life and safety of persons. And in the absence of any further argument from Shawn, or anyone else, locking up the tiger seems to be no less just (and perhaps a great deal more just) than letting the tiger roam free to attack other persons. In short, the normative conclusion Shawn attempts to draw from his factual premise just does not follow necessarily, even if you assume the factual premise to be true.

Second, the premise of Shawn's argument implies a broader rule, which he has left unstated. It would be this, or something close to this:

> It is always unjust to punish a person or to inflict revenge on him or her if (1) that person committed an illegal (or immoral) act and (2) we cannot determine that they could have done otherwise (that they had a free choice in the matter).

So, his complete argument is:

It is always unjust to punish a person or to inflict revenge on a person if (1) that person committed an illegal (or immoral) act and (2) we cannot determine that he or she could have done otherwise. [An implied first premise, a general rule]

There's absolutely no way to determine that the person being punished, or the person against whom revenge is taken, [for committing an illegal or immoral act] was capable of behaving differently from the way they behaved. [Shawn's premise]

[Therefore], punishment and revenge are unjust. [Shawn's conclusion]

Now, in light of our discussion of factual and normative statements, what do you notice about the first premise? It is a normative statement ("it is always unjust . . .").

So, Shawn's reconstructed argument can be restated so that he is not guilty of drawing a normative conclusion solely from a factual premise. Rather, he appears to be attempting to draw a normative conclusion from a normative premise (the implied general rule) and a factual premise (his actually stated premise).

That sort of argument, in itself, is not a problem from a logical or argumentative point of view. People make such arguments all the time in normal moral and legal discourse. For example, you might argue to a friend:

Jones is a murderer.
Therefore, Jones has done a morally wrong act.

The conclusion, however, does not follow from the premise alone. It follows from the premise only if an implied general rule also is part of the argument, namely, "Murder is always morally wrong." The complete argument, then, is:

Murder is always morally wrong.
Jones is a murderer.
Therefore, Jones has done a morally wrong act.

To return to Shawn's argument, he is asking us to commit to the truth of his unstated normative premise—"It is always unjust to punish a person or to inflict revenge on a person if (1) that person committed an illegal (or immoral) act and (2) we cannot determine that he or she could have done otherwise." But he offers no argument in support of it.

Maybe you accept this normative statement as true without argument or maybe you do not. *The important point here is that the reader is not compelled to accept the truth of Shawn's normative conclusion until the truth of the normative premise has been accepted, either without further argument or as proven by further argument.* (Note that a complete argument by Shawn for his conclusion would also require that he justify his factual premise, and he would need some facts or other evidence to establish that.)

Example 2. Advances in medicine and biology have created moral issues that did not exist for your grandparents or their grandparents. Among these advances are the ability to implant a human embryo in a woman who is not the biological mother of the embryo to allow the embryo to develop and be carried to full term. The woman who carries the embryo is known as the surrogate mother and the entire process is known as gestational surrogacy (or, for our purposes here, simply surrogacy). One of the moral and legal issues surrounding surrogacy is whether the surrogate mother should be paid for her services. State laws in the United States take different approaches to paid surrogacy. Accordingly, you can find many opinion pieces on this issue in newspapers, magazines, and online. Any one of them may argue along these lines:

> There is nothing more wonderful than parenthood. Yet many loving couples cannot have children of their own. Infertility is widespread in some countries and among some populations. That prevents many heterosexual couples from conceiving or carrying a healthy baby to term. Many male homosexual couples want a child that is biologically related to one of the partners. For many heterosexual and homosexual couples, surrogacy is the only path to parenthood.
>
> Not surprisingly, few women are willing to volunteer to be surrogates, especially for complete strangers. Pregnancy may involve substantial risks to the heath of the woman carrying the fetus, and it can involve other ailments, such as morning sickness, sleepless nights, and chronic back or nerve pain.
>
> Our federal government ought to promote loving family units. Society benefits in numerous ways from stable, loving families. Numerous studies have shown that when adults are part of loving families, they are happier than childless couples or single people. In the current environment in which there is a scarcity of volunteer surrogates and rising demand, and a patchwork of state laws governing surrogacy, our national Congress should enact a national law encouraging surrogacy by permitting surrogates to be paid for their services, in addition to compensation for their expenses. Doctors and nurses get paid to provide health-related services. By the same token, surrogates should be paid for their health-related services.
>
> Being a parent is a joyful experience with many social benefits that extend across the nation. Accordingly, our federal government should encourage parenthood by enacting a national law permitting and regulating paid surrogacy.

The next-to-the-last paragraph of this text is a good place to start our analysis. That paragraph contains this argument:

There is a scarcity of volunteer surrogate mothers. [Premise]
There is a rising demand for surrogate mothers. [Premise]
Paying surrogate mothers for their services will increase the number of women willing to serve as surrogates. [Implied premise]
Paying surrogate mothers is morally unobjectionable [implied conclusion] because:
Doctors and nurses get paid to provide health-related services. [Subpremise]
Surrogate mothers provide health-related services. [Subpremise]
Our federal government ought to promote loving family units. [Premise]
Society benefits in numerous ways from stable, loving families. [Subpremise]
Numerous studies have shown that when adults are part of loving families, they are happier than childless couples or single people. [Subpremise]
[Therefore,] our federal government should encourage parenthood by enacting a national law permitting and regulating paid surrogacy. [Conclusion]

Now, does this final normative conclusion follow logically from the premises? If the premises are true, does the conclusion follow with necessity (as in a valid deductive argument), with a high probability (as in a strong inductive argument), or neither? What normative commitments does this argument require the reader to accept?

Let's begin to answer these questions by examining the first subargument embedded in this larger argument.

Doctors and nurses get paid to provide health-related services. [Subpremise]
Surrogate mothers provide health-related services. [Subpremise]
[Therefore,] paying surrogate mothers is morally unobjectionable. [Implied conclusion]

As stated, the two factual subpremises do not logically support the normative conclusion. There is no way to reason simply from the fact that someone provides health-related services to a moral conclusion. The author can draw that moral conclusion only by assuming an implied normative subpremise, as follows:

It is morally unobjectionable for doctors and nurses to be paid to provide health-related services. [Implied subpremise]

With the addition of this implied normative subpremise, the argument reasons by analogy: that the delivery of health-related services by doctors and nurses is similar to a surrogate's delivery of health-related services, and just as the former is morally unobjectionable, so too is the latter.

Whether that inductive argument by analogy is strong or weak depends on the ways in which the delivery of health-related services by doctors and nurses, on the one hand, is similar to or distinct from the delivery of those types of services by a surrogate, on the other hand. (We discussed arguments by analogy in chapter 4.) Recognizing the need for the implied normative premise highlights the argument's commitment to these services being sufficiently similar that the normative conclusion follows from the stated and implied subpremises.

Let's consider the second subargument in this paragraph:

Society benefits in numerous ways from stable families.
Numerous studies have shown that when adults are part of loving families, they are happier than childless couples or single people.
[Therefore,] our federal government actively ought to promote loving family units.

Does the normative conclusion follow logically from these factual premises?

No. The factual premises are about the benefits to society and the happiness of adults. There is no logical step that gets you from those two premises alone to a conclusion about what our federal government ought to do. To see this, note that these premises equally well (or equally poorly) support (a) the more neutral conclusion that the federal government actively "ought not discourage" loving family units, rather than the conclusion stated, or (b) that our state or local governments, rather than the federal government, actively ought to promote loving family units.

More directly, this subargument assumes an unstated normative premise, something like this:

The federal government has a duty to promote social benefits and the happiness of its citizens.

Many books and articles have been written in support of and opposed to this statement, not to mention that many wars have been fought over it. Perhaps, instead, our national government ought to promote liberty, adherence to a particular religious doctrine, unfettered capitalism, or some other value, rather than whatever someone may deem to be "social benefits" or "happiness." You may be willing to accept this unstated premise or not, but it is important to recognize that this subargument asks you to commit to it.

It is productive to step back and look at the normative-factual distinction from a broader perspective. As we discussed in example 1 above, to assess an argument that purports to draw a normative conclusion from factual premises, it is often useful to ask whether any counterexample(s) show that the conclusion does not follow from the premises. The argument on surrogacy is an inductive argument, so the introduction of additional facts can show the argument to be weaker than may first appear.

Suppose, hypothetically, you were to learn that there are 10 million orphans in the United States, living on the streets, in orphanages, or in foster homes. If that were true, then rather than encouraging surrogate births, perhaps our federal government should encourage infertile or homosexual couples to adopt children already born. Perhaps the government actively should discourage the birth of more children. Perhaps the federal government has a stronger duty to prevent the unnecessary suffering of already living orphaned children than to encourage the births of more children.

Similarly, suppose the topic of this essay was not surrogacy, but rather organ donations. In the United States, payment for organ donation is prohibited. Suppose a very poor woman is willing to sell one of her kidneys to get money to feed her family, but she would not be willing to donate one for free. Should a national law be enacted that allows her to be paid? Or, should she be prohibited from getting paid for that? Does payment for an organ allow rich couples to exploit poor women and encourage them to undertake avoidable health-related risks, but surrogacy does not? Or, do both procedures exploit poor women? Or, do both procedures simply allow for a free economic exchange that makes both parties better off?

In short, if the laws prohibiting compensation for being an organ donor are grounded in a normative (moral) rule (e.g., the rich should not exploit the poor), why does that same rule not also lead to the conclusion that surrogate mothers should be prohibited from being compensated for their services? If it does apply, then the preceding argument that the federal government should enact a law that permits compensation for being a surrogate mother looks a lot less strong. There may be good arguments for the conclusion that we should have a national law permitting compensation for surrogate mothers, but the question you must ask is whether this essay has made them and, if so, what normative commitments does it require you to make?

Much more could be said about the normative-factual distinction. We have said enough, however, to provide you with this tool for your toolbox: *the distinction between factual and normative statements allows you to understand that (1) normative conclusions cannot be drawn from purely factual premises, (2) when an author is arguing for a normative conclusion, he usually is asking you, the reader, to accept other express or implied normative statements, and (3) the author may, or may not, assert arguments in support of those other statements.*

In sum, political or social opinion pieces—especially when they are advocating for some normative position, as they typically are—need to be read with care. The point is not that the positions they stake out can never be proven or are never persuasive. Rather, you will greatly benefit from analyzing such pieces to understand the factual assumptions and the moral, legal, or other normative assumptions they make or that they assume you accept. Meaningful and productive debate over normative conclusions requires an understanding as to their factual and normative foundations—and that requires digging down to reveal those foundations.

Irony: Saying What You Do Not Mean

Sometimes a phrase or a sentence is odd or puzzling, at least at first glance, because it is used to communicate a thought that is the opposite of what the words literally say. "Irony" is the use of words to convey a meaning that is the opposite of, or at least that markedly differs from, the usual, literal meaning of those words.[3]

Undoubtedly, you have heard the terms "irony" or "ironic" many times. They are commonly bandied about in popular culture (movies, TV, articles in the mass media) and in everyday speech ("I was being ironic . . ."). Irony is such a common modern form of writing and speaking that being able to recognize it and understand how it is used is often essential to understanding what you are reading. So, it will be useful to spend some time discussing it here.

Writers usually use irony to emphasize a point. You have already seen one example of irony, in our ice cream example in chapter 1. The first two sentences of that example are, "Dude, it's summer. It's hot and humid—news flash." The second half of the second sentence—"news flash"—is a use of irony. What your friend is trying to communicate in the first two sentences is that it is obvious and to be expected that it will be hot and humid in the summer. The phrase "news flash" literally means the opposite of that. She is using "news flash" to communicate the opposite of the usual, literal meaning of those words.

Let's consider some additional simple examples.

Suppose you live in a city in a northern climate, it is mid-February, you have had a brutal winter with excessive amounts of snow, and everyone is feeling the midwinter blues. You might say to a friend, "Gosh, I hope it snows today!" The literal meaning of those words, of course, is that you want it to snow today. The meaning you are trying to express, however, is the opposite of that—you do not want it to snow today. That is an ironic statement.

Suppose Smith, a notorious murderer, dies in prison. You hear a commentator on TV saying, "I'm sure there's a special place in heaven for Smith." The commentator really means that there is a special place in hell for Smith.

Suppose you run into a friend on the street who you have not seen for a while. You ask her how things are going. She responds, "Great. Couldn't be any better. I'm flunking two of my courses, my dog got killed by a car last week, my mother has threatened not to pay my tuition next semester, and I'm having some serious medical problems." In light of your friend's list of woes, it is not hard to spot the ironic statements here—"Great. Couldn't be any better."

Rhetoric

In the discussion of rhetoric in chapter 4, you read about rhetorical statements, questions, and passages. It will be useful to elaborate on that discussion to show how rhetoric is distinct from mere factual statements and how rhetorical statements may appear factual when they are, instead, making normative claims.

Dr. King's "Letter from a Birmingham Jail"[4] contains many famous rhetorical statements. Before we consider them, a bit of background is helpful. In 1963 Dr. King was arrested for his participation in nonviolent civil rights protests in Birmingham, Alabama. He wrote this essay, styled as a "letter," while in jail in Birmingham. The essay is a response to a public statement signed by eight white clergymen who, in effect, publicly asked Dr. King, "why are you, a clergyman from Atlanta, Georgia, coming to Birmingham, Alabama, to demonstrate in our streets and cause problems?" Dr. King's response is a classic defense of illegal nonviolent protest and is a classic of the twentieth-century Civil Rights Movement in the United States.

Consider these oft-quoted sentences from this essay.

> We are caught in an inescapable network of mutuality, tied together in a single garment of destiny. Whatever affects one directly, affects all indirectly. (Paragraph 4)

Dr. King is trying to make a moral point here. He effectively declares, "I'm here protesting because injustice is not merely a local problem. It affects everyone." Yet Dr. King's rhetoric makes this point more powerfully through metaphors of "networks of mutuality" and "a single garment of destiny."

Dr. King could have stated his moral point more directly like this, "The duty to fight injustice does not stop at state lines and is not limited to citizens of the state in which the injustice occurs." But notice how this restatement lacks the expansiveness and grandeur of Dr. King's rhetorical flourishes. Dr. King's two sentences have the ring of eternal moral truths, whereas this restatement tends to be closer to a dry legal claim about state borders.

A rhetorical question is a question that is asked to make a point and is not usually a question that the author or speaker expects to be answered. Recall Dr. King's rhetorical question at the beginning of his sermon, "Antidotes for fear," which we considered in chapter 5. He did not ask, "what is fear?" or simply state, "Everyone everywhere lives in fear." Rather, with rhetorical flair, he asks:

> In these days of *catastrophic change* and *calamitous uncertainty*, is there any man who does not experience the *depression* and *bewilderment* of *crippling fear*, which, like a *nagging hound of hell, pursues our every footstep*? (Emphases added.)

The literal meaning of the question is that everyone lives in fear all the time. Through his rhetorical question, however, Dr. King also is telling his congregation, "I know what's going on in your hearts and minds—fear—because it's going on in mine as well. Here's how I have been thinking about it and trying to deal with it, and you can too." That is powerful because it says to the audience, "we are in this together, and here's my contribution to the dialogue going on in your mind."

Suppose this sermon began with this question, "Why is fear so widespread in our society?" or with the declarative statement, "Everyone everywhere lives in fear all of the time." Those may be good ways to start an essay in an academic psychology or sociology journal, but they are not going to grip anyone's heartstrings and they do not communicate that this sermon is important to anyone as a practical matter in living their everyday lives. In speaking to his congregation, communicating the importance of the topic of the sermon undoubtedly is part what Dr. King wanted to do. So, he loaded his question with rhetorical terms ("catastrophic change," "calamitous uncertainty," "nagging hound of hell") which grip the emotions and communicate that this sermon has practical importance. That use of rhetorical terms communicates even more powerfully that mastering fear is practically important because fear inescapably and relentlessly chases after you like a mad hound from hell.

An entire paragraph consisting almost entirely of nonrhetorical, declarative sentences can be rhetorical. Such sentences, in the hands of a skilled writer, can be combined into an anecdote of considerable rhetorical power. Consider this anecdote by the Pulitzer Prize winning columnist Brent A. Staples in his essay, "Black Men and Public Spaces":

> My first victim was a woman—white, well-dressed, probably in her late twenties. I came upon her late one evening on a deserted street in Hyde Park, a relatively affluent neighborhood in an otherwise mean, impoverished section of Chicago. As I swung onto the avenue behind her, there seemed to be a discreet, uninflammatory distance between us. Not so. She cast back a worried glance. To her, the youngish black man—a broad six feet two inches with a beard and billowing hair . . . —seemed menacingly close. After a few more quick glimpses, she picked up her pace and was soon running in earnest. Within seconds, she disappeared into a cross street.[5]

Staples builds great suspense with this paragraph. It starts with his use of "victim." In what way was this woman his "victim"? What did he do when she went around the corner onto a cross street? Where is this essay going? What is his point? This introductory paragraph grabs our attention and compels us to keep reading. Staples uses this story to illustrate how he came to recognize his ability, as a young African American man, "to alter public space in ugly ways."

Being able to spot and understand nonfactual, nonliteral uses of language—normative statements, irony, and rhetoric—is an essential tool for wrestling the meaning out of argumentative texts. These nonfactual uses of language are sometimes parts of an argument and sometimes have a more or less direct relation to the argument. Theoretic arguments relating to certain subject matters will tend to consist solely of factual statements. For example, a theoretic argument about the nature of gravity is unlikely to contain any normative statements, irony, or rhetoric. On the other hand, a theoretical argument on a moral issue may consist of both factual and normative statements, as we saw in Wallace Shawn's theoretical argument on punishment. Dr. King's theoretic argument on civil disobedience consists of factual, normative, and rhetorical statements. Practical arguments will almost certainly expressly or implicitly contain at least one normative statement, since such arguments are expressions of what a person or entity should do based on some value.

Determining the relationship among the statements that constitute an argument and the other parts of a text is often a matter of judgment, especially when the author's argument is not clear or is embedded deeply within a text thick with one of the nonfactual uses of language examined here. Once you have come to such an initial determination for any text, ask yourself whether it is within the zone of reasonableness we discussed in chapter 3. If so, great. If not, go back to the text and try again. You *can* do it.

NOTES

1. You probably have seen him on TV or in a movie, even if you do not recognize his name. Check out en.wikipedia.org/wiki/Wallace_Shawn.

2. Wallace Shawn, *Night Thoughts*, p. 59 (Chicago: Haymarket Books 2017).

3. Irony is closely related to sarcasm, but they are not the same. Like irony, sarcasm often uses words that say one thing to mean their opposite or something very different. It differs from irony in that it is often critical of a person or situation or is biting commentary, while ironic statements do not need to be either. Also, sarcasm need not use words to say the opposite of what they literally mean. For example, if a person is going to proceed with some action that was a major failure the first time he tried it, his friend might say (with a sneering tone of voice), "Okay, and how did that work out for you before?"

4. Available at, africa.upenn.edu/Articles_Gen/Letter_Birmingham.html. You can find several versions of this essay online, with both substantive and stylistic variations.

5. Brent A. Staples, "Black Men and Public Spaces," in *Harper's*, December 1986.

Chapter 8

Context Imparts Meaning

You think your pain and heartbreak are unprecedented in the history of the world, but then you read. It was Dostoevsky and Dickens who taught me that the things that tormented me were the very things that connected me with all the people who were alive, or who have ever been alive. —James Baldwin (African American essayist, 1924–1987, interview in *LIFE* magazine, May 24, 1963)

Some college and university professors teach that if you want to fully understand an argumentative text, all you need to do is to read the text. And to gain a deeper understanding of it, reread it, and reread it again, and so on. So, for example, if you want to understand one of Sigmund Freud's monographs (his actual work, and not a summary of that monograph and not a textbook rehash of what Freud thought), then read the book. And because Freud is difficult to understand, reread it as many times as needed until you do understand it. Perhaps you are attending one of those colleges, and perhaps your professors have taught you that lesson. And, because you are trying to be a diligent student, perhaps you followed their instruction.

What were the results of these efforts? Very likely, terrible. You will have spent a lot of time spinning your wheels and going in circles like a dog chasing its tail. Why? Because the really interesting and difficult texts you will read are invariably part of a conversation, a dialogue, a debate, sometimes one stretching across centuries. And you will not really appreciate why an author is making this argument or that, or taking this approach or that, or why the work is revolutionary or a mere rehash of common knowledge until you have some knowledge of that extended conversation, or at least the principal topics and issues being discussed in that dialogue.

Think of reading any great book (or, sometimes, even a common essay in a newspaper's editorial pages) as the equivalent of walking into a movie about halfway through. (In college you may hear this situation expressed by the Latin phrase *in medias res*—in the middle of things.) There is a lot of catching up to do, and your understanding of the part of the movie you are watching will be limited because you have not seen the first half. You may have trouble figuring out the relationship of the characters, why they are doing what they are doing, the plot, and so on. In the first scene that *you* see, the plot unfolds that Martha is having Joe's baby. So what? Who is Martha? Who is Joe? Why is this important? How will this affect them, the other characters, or the outcome of the story?

"Read (and reread) only the text you have in front of you"—the lesson too many students have learned too well—is the equivalent of watching that movie from the same midpoint to the end multiple times. Do you think that will give you any better insights into what happened in the first half-hour or hour of the movie? Undoubtedly, you will pick up bits and pieces, but nothing like having watched the complete movie, not the full plot of the movie.

So, at some point, after a lot of frustration, you may have come to the realization, "I'm getting nowhere." If you had that epiphany, or are working toward it, here is what you need to do: ignore what you have been taught and begin to read everything you can to place your assigned readings into a context that allows you to better understand them.

In this chapter we are going to discuss how context gives meaning to an argumentative text. We are going to focus principally on intellectual, social, political, cultural context, since you will most often need to understand how these may enrich the meaning of reading argumentative texts. We also will consider briefly how the physical environment may act as context giving meaning to a text.

INTELLECTUAL CONTEXT

Most argumentative texts (and virtually all scholarly argumentative texts) are attempts to respond to other arguments made by other authors to address a question, problem, or issue. They are part of an ongoing, multiperson dialogue. We can call the dialogue or debate in which an argumentative text is participating the intellectual context of that text.

The first place to look for the intellectual context of an argumentative text is within the text itself. Sometimes the author expressly states that her work is responding to the work of another author on the same problem. Sometimes the author only implicitly acknowledges that her work is a response to the arguments of another on the topic.

Those other arguments may have been made centuries ago or may be contemporaneous with those the author is making. As an example of the former, scholars are still studying Aristotle's *Nicomachean Ethics* (written over 2,000 years ago) and answering its arguments as to the nature of happiness and virtue. As an example of the latter, on any given day you can pick up the editorial page of a newspaper and see one or more opinion pieces that effectively are part of a conversation about the nature of a good society, what rights citizens do and do not have (a right to health care?), and the limits of freedom and the power of government (does the government have a right to tap your phone? track your location?). Some of those arguments are made side by side with articles taking the opposite point of view, or they are reactions to opinion pieces written a day or week before.

More specifically, the text itself often will provide you with guides to its intellectual context by explicitly or implicitly stating what arguments or positions it is responding to or disputing, what dialogue it is participating in. You may see this in the form of a statement in the text like this, "There is a school of thought [or a scholar, Ms. A] that believes X. In this essay, I will prove that X is incorrect [or only partially correct]. And I will show that Y [an alternative] is correct."

Dr. King's "Letter from a Birmingham Jail"[1] is a good example of an author's self-conscious participation in a dialogue. It expressly is a response to a statement written by eight white clergymen that criticized Dr. King for conducting nonviolent civil rights protests in Birmingham. It begins:

> While confined here in the Birmingham city jail, I came across your recent statement calling my present activities "unwise and untimely." Seldom do I pause to answer criticism of my work and ideas. . . . But since I feel that you are men of genuine good will and that your criticisms are sincerely set forth, I want to try to answer your statement in what I hope will be patient and reasonable terms.

In the remainder of the essay, Dr. King addresses the many criticisms made by the clergymen.

You will find an important variation on this way of providing intellectual context when an author states that she is taking a position that is a response to *the lack of an argument or lack of a conclusion* by others. This is the "up to now we have been living in ignorance" form of response. It is just as much part of an ongoing dialogue as an essay in which the opponent's position is expressly identified. You will see this, for example, in this sort of statement:

> For years social scientists have been studying the causes of urban poverty. They have pointed to four main causes: (1) . . ., (2) . . ., (3) . . ., and (4) . . . . No one, however, has yet examined how urban poverty is caused by X. In this paper I will demonstrate that X is the only cause of urban poverty. [In other words, "Up to now, until this paper was published, we have been living in ignorance of the real cause."]

Notwithstanding that this essay purports to be staking out a whole new causal analysis, the argument is still part of the ongoing conversation as to the causes of urban poverty; it recognizes and is implicitly rejecting or refining all of the previously stated views on the causes. The author's statement of the prior work of the social scientists studying this problem provides intellectual context for his purportedly groundbreaking work.

A notable example of this "up to now we have been living in ignorance" approach is found in John Stuart Mill's 1861 classic in moral philosophy, *Utilitarianism*:

> There are few circumstances among those which make up the present condition of human knowledge . . . more significant of *the backward state* in which speculation on the most important subjects still lingers, than *the little progress* which has been made in the decision of the controversy respecting the criterion of right and wrong.[2]

Mill then refers to one of Plato's works, written more than two thousand years previously, in which Plato articulates and rejects the moral theory Mill propounds in his work.

When the content of a text itself provides you with intellectual context by expressly or implicitly addressing arguments of another author or school of thought, that points you to another source for understanding the text you are reading—namely, the works of that other author or school of thought. If an author, Mr. X, is stating that he is responding to the arguments of Ms. Y, you will better understand Mr. X's argument if you go back and read what Ms. Y had to say on the same issue. Is Mr. X accurately portraying what Ms. Y wrote on the issue, her arguments and conclusions? Has Mr. X really offered a better analysis of the problem than Ms. Y? If you read Ms. Y's writing on the subject, you will have a far better understanding of the dialogue of which Mr. X's argument is a part.

Let's go back to our movie analogy. Suppose the movie you are watching has an intermission (or the device you are watching it on has a pause button). And suppose you meet a good friend during the intermission and she explains the plot, who the characters are, what happened so far in the movie, and so on. With that intellectual context, you will have a far better understanding of what you are watching from that point on. With respect to argumentative texts, there are several additional sources to turn to that perform the same function as your friend explaining the first of half the movie, to give the part of the movie you are watching context.

To begin with two obvious sources, teachers and friends can perform this function, to a greater or lesser extent. Reach out to them. Tap their knowledge.

Secondary sources also perform the function of your friend at intermission, and typically with far more rigor and insight. A secondary source is any book or article that interprets or criticizes another book or article, which is the primary source you are focused on. For example, Thomas Nagel's essay, "Rawls on Justice," is a secondary source interpreting John Rawls' classic philosophical treatise, *A Theory of Justice*. Or to use a hypothetical example, a book titled *Freud's Radical View of the Mind* would be a secondary source interpreting or criticizing Sigmund Freud's theory of human psychology.

Secondary sources "open up" the meaning of primary texts by emphasizing key arguments in the primary text, explaining why these or those points are important, and, perhaps most usefully, explaining why the author is taking the approach he is, why he is making certain arguments and the significance of those arguments relative to the other works that are part of the same ongoing conversation. In the terms of our movie analogy, secondary sources allow you to understand why it is a big deal that Martha is having Joe's baby.

SOCIAL, POLITICAL, AND CULTURAL CONTEXT

In addition to intellectual context, there are more diffuse and more amorphous social, political, and cultural contexts of a text. When an author intentionally employs one of these contexts, he expressly or implicitly refers to the social, political, or cultural circumstances in which a text is written to import into the text the meanings that the audience associates with those circumstances. Those circumstances may be historical or contemporaneous with the text.

Further, a reader may refer to the social, political, and cultural contexts of a text to give it meaning even when an author does not intentionally use such contexts. A reader might read a work written in the eighteenth century, for example, and conclude, "this work is infused with all of the main themes of the French Enlightenment." Another reader may read Freud's psychological treatises and come to the view that "Freud's views on sex are a product of the morality of the upper classes in Victorian England."

Consider this example of social and cultural context. In early 1860, Abraham Lincoln traveled to New York and delivered a speech on slavery and the possible dissolution of the Union over the issue of slavery. We now refer to that speech colloquially as the "House Divided" speech because of Lincoln's famous line, "A house divided against itself cannot stand. I believe this government cannot endure, permanently half slave and half free."

We understand more profoundly the meaning of this metaphor of "a house divided" and the power of Lincoln's use of it when we understand its social and cultural context. Lincoln was echoing the passage in the Gospel of Matthew in which Christ rejected the criticism that he cast out demons (devils) through the power of the Devil by declaring, "Every kingdom divided against itself is brought to desolation; and every city or house divided against itself shall not stand. And if Satan cast out Satan, he is divided against himself; how shall then his kingdom stand?"[3] To a largely Christian audience raised on reading the New Testament, Lincoln's "house divided" metaphor rooted his views on slavery and politics in widely and deeply held religious beliefs, and hence gave those views additional rhetorical force and authority.

When Dr. King was a freshman in college, he read and was greatly influenced by the 1849 essay of the transcendentalist writer Henry David Thoreau, "Civil Disobedience."[4] In that essay, Thoreau recalls a night he spent in jail for an act of nonviolent civil disobedience—not paying a tax that supported the Mexican War, which he strongly opposed. The essay is the seminal modern work defending nonviolent civil disobedience as a means of protest against injustice.

Does knowing this give us any deeper insight into why Dr. King framed his classic defense of civil disobedience, "Letter from a Birmingham Jail," as an essay written in a jail? Even without researching the issue, Thoreau's influence on Dr. King strongly suggests that Dr. King is consciously framing his defense of civil disobedience as a letter from a jail to place it within a time-honored strain of American political thought.

Recall that in chapter 2 we discussed that when you first pick up a book, the table of contents, the preface, the back page, and so on may provide context for the text of particular chapters. Not to be overlooked, among the types of political or cultural context is the publication or publishing house in which the text appears. This may suggest the political or cultural biases of the text. An essay in the *National Review* or *Wall Street Journal*, for example, is more likely to have a conservative slant, while an essay in *Mother Jones* or *The Nation* is likely to have a liberal slant. Certain publishing houses of books have similar political leanings. Haymarket Books, for example, leans to the left (liberal) side of the political spectrum, while Regnery Publishing touts itself as publishing "great conservative books." Online publications similarly often have political or cultural leanings that point to the similar perspectives of their authors.

Different types of context—intellectual, social, cultural, or political—will be most useful for understanding the meaning of different types of texts. If you are reading a current editorial on free speech on college campuses, for example, you may find the current political or social context of the piece of most use. If you are reading the work of a modern philosopher on the proper limits of free speech in society in general, you may find it most helpful to understand the prior arguments of philosophers on this issue, going back decades or centuries. You will get better at finding useful sources for providing the appropriate context as you better understand the challenges to understanding that the argumentative text you are reading presents.

PHYSICAL ENVIRONMENT AS CONTEXT

You often will not need to consider the physical environment as providing context in your reading of an argumentative text, but you do need to be aware of it. Indeed, we have already encountered in this book an example of how the physical environment may provide context, and yet you could easily have read the text without recognizing this.

Recall the ice cream example in the beginning of chapter 1. You texted a friend complaining about the heat and humidity and she texted this reply:

> Dude, it's summer. It's hot and humid—news flash. You want to cool off. Eat some ice cream. You'll feel like an April day, like springtime. The store's across the street from you. They have Cosmic Mix, your favorite flavor. If you want to try something new, go for Cherry Berry, my favorite.

Recall also that we examined two possible meanings that your friend may intend by this sentence: "The store's across the street from you." Those meanings depend on what your friend knows about that street.

The other side of this coin is that the meaning *you* give to the sentence depends on what you believe your friend knows about your physical environment when she sent her text. If you believe your friend knows that the street is a quiet two-lane street, then you will interpret that sentence to mean something like, "It's not inconvenient or a risk for you to go to the store." If you believe your friend knows that the street is a heavily trafficked six-lane boulevard with no traffic signals and a forty-mile-per-hour speed limit, then you will take her sentence to mean something like, "Going to the store and eating ice cream is worth risking your life and limb." In short, the physical environment that an author knows or assumes can provide context for her text, giving one meaning or another to her statements about that environment.

What about the situation in which you do not know what your friend knows about the street? Maybe you have never been on this street with your friend, or you believe she is getting her information from a sketchy online source, or you are not sure whether she has a fuzzy memory of where you are, and so on. If you do not have a firm belief about what your friend knows about the street—or more generally, about your physical environment—the meaning of her sentence will be ambiguous and you just cannot determine which reasonable interpretation she intends.

Of course, presumably you could call her up or text her back for clarification, as we often do in these situations. But until you get her response, if ever, you do not have a belief about what she knows about your physical environment that allows you to attribute one meaning to her sentence to the exclusion of the other. (If you were to summarize her text (or any similar text), you would simply note the ambiguity and state that the author's meaning is uncertain.)

Some serious texts may require you to probe an author's beliefs or assumptions about the physical environment of her subjects in order to understand what she means. Suppose you are reading a text about the battle of Gettysburg in the Civil War or the Battle of the Bulge in World War II. Suppose, further, that the author made a claim that referenced the physical characteristics of the battlefield. The author may have written, for example, "General X ignored the first rule of military engagements, 'Always secure the high ground,' and flanked his forces to the north." The meaning you give to that statement may depend on what you believe the author knows about the geography of the battlefield in which General X was fighting. You may interpret the statement to be critical if the author has discussed a hilltop that General X failed to secure. You may interpret the statement as neutral or merely descriptive if the author previously noted that the battlefield terrain was flat, so that General X had no need to follow this "first rule."

NOTES

1. Available at africa.upenn.edu/Articles_Gen/Letter_Birmingham.html.

2. Chap. I, first paragraph (Indianapolis: Hackett Publishing 1979, George Sher, ed.) (emphases added).

3. Matthew 12:25–26, King James Version. Similarly, the famous opening phrase of the *Gettysburg Address*, "Fourscore and seven years ago . . .," echoes Psalm 90, verse 10 of the Old Testament (also referred to as the Hebrew Bible).

4. *The Autobiography of Martin Luther King, Jr.,* p. 14 (New York: Warner Books 1998, Clayborne Carson, ed.).

Chapter 9

The ABCs of Logic

Read anything you want. Just read. Books are possibilities. They are escape routes. They give you options when you have none. Each can be a home for an uprooted mind.—Matt Haig, *Reasons to Stay Alive*, p. 242 (London: Canongate 2016)

As we discussed in chapter 4, deductive arguments may be valid or invalid and inductive arguments may be strong or weak. There are many ways for an argument to be invalid or weak, but some logical errors are so common that over the years they have been singled out and given names. In the first section of this chapter we will look at a few of the more common errors in reasoning. In the second section we will discuss the distinction between necessary and sufficient conditions and address why that distinction is so important.

This chapter is just the very beginning of a course on logic. It provides just a few of the tools you will find useful in reading for understanding. There are many resources available for you to educate yourself further on the various forms of errors in reasoning and rules that govern valid arguments. These will enable you to better analyze and understand argumentative texts.

INFORMAL LOGIC: COMMON FALLACIES

A *fallacy* is a common error in reasoning. There are many types of fallacies. We will discuss here a few of the typical ones that you are likely to have encountered and likely will encounter.

Equivocation (ambiguity). The fallacy of equivocation occurs when the author (or speaker) gives a critical word or phrase in the premises of an argument two different meanings and draws a conclusion from those premises that is possible only because of the ambiguity in the critical term or phrase.

Consider a variation on our Socrates example:

Socrates was a horse.
Socrates was a great philosopher.
Therefore, at least one horse was a great philosopher.

This deductive argument is invalid. It commits the fallacy of equivocation because in the first premise "Socrates" refers to a horse (say, someone in Kentucky named his favorite horse "Socrates") and in the second premise "Socrates" refers to a person (the ancient Greek philosopher Socrates who taught Plato). "Socrates" is ambiguous because it has two different meanings (refers to two different things). From this equivocation on the word "Socrates," one then draws the false conclusion that there has been one horse who was a great philosopher. If it is true that someone named his horse "Socrates" and if the ancient Greek person named "Socrates" was a great philosopher, it does not necessarily follow that at least one horse was a great philosopher.

The two premises have no logical connection. The "Socrates" in the first premise has nothing to do with the "Socrates" in the second premise, and so that term cannot make the connection between the first and second premises that necessarily leads to the conclusion.

Suppose, however, that "Socrates" refers to the same animal (the same thing) in both premises—a horse or a person. Would the argument still be invalid? No. Then the argument would be valid. Why?

Suppose "Socrates" refers to a horse. Then the second premise is false (no horse can be a philosopher, of course). But remember, all that it takes for an argument to be valid is that *if* the premises are true, the conclusion necessarily follows. And here, *if* "Socrates" refers to a horse in both premises, and *if* the second premise is true, then the conclusion necessarily follows. Likewise, assume that "Socrates" refers to a person in both premises. Then the first premise would be false, but *if* it were true, then the conclusion necessarily follows, and so the argument is valid. That may sound a bit nutty, but remember, the validity of a deductive argument is distinct from the truth or falsity of any one of its premises or its conclusion.

Consider these additional examples of equivocation.

Good workers are hard to find.
You want to hire a good worker.
So, you need to look where they are hiding.

The ambiguous phrase is "hard to find." Read literally, it means that something is hidden or lost in an unknown place. Read as a figure of speech, it means uncommon or rare.

Here is an old joke that depends on the fallacy of equivocation:

Doctor: Mr. Jones, I'm sorry to tell you that you have a fatal disease.
Mr. Jones: That's terrible. I'd like a second opinion.
Doctor: Okay, you're ugly.

"A second opinion," literally means an opinion in addition to the first opinion, which is how the doctor interprets the phrase. As a figure of speech, it means an opinion from a second doctor on the patient's medical condition.

Consider this one, which is updated from a passage in Lewis Carroll's *Through the Looking-Glass*:

Bobby: I heard you drove to Dubuque on July 4th. Nobody travels on the 4th of July, so I'm sure you had an easy drive.
Jimmy: Bobby, the roads were packed when I drove on the 4th of July. But I didn't see Nobody. So, I guess he was traveling on a different highway than I was.

When Bobby says "Nobody," he means no one, not any person. When Jimmy says "Nobody" he means a person named "Nobody" and from that he draws a conclusion ("So, I guess he was . . .") that does not follow from the premises.

Begging the question (or circular reasoning). You commonly hear in the media or common conversation, "well, that begs the question whether . . ." That use of the phrase "begs the question" means "invites the question," "raises the question," or "leads us to ask the question." That use of the phrase is relatively new (and, arguably, reflects a misunderstanding of the phrase). There is no logical fallacy involved when someone "begs the question" in this sense. So, that is not the sense of "begging the question" we are concerned with here.

Traditionally, "to beg the question" or "begging the question" refers to an argument in which the premises do not provide independent proof of a conclusion (the question), but rather state or restate the very conclusion that they are supposed to prove. The premises do not answer a question (prove a conclusion), but rather state the question in some other way. So, when you beg the question, you are arguing in a circle. To beg the question is this sense is to commit a logical fallacy. This is the sense of "begging the question" we are concerned with here.

Let's begin with an obvious example:

Women shouldn't be allowed to join the Army because only men should be allowed to join the Army.

To put this in a more formal structure:

Only men should be allowed to join the Army.
Therefore, women shouldn't be allowed to join the Army.

The conclusion restates the premise by stating that women should not be allowed to do what only men should be allowed to do. The premise does not provide an independent reason for the conclusion.

Here is a common example of begging the question:

God exists because the Bible says he exists and the Bible is the inspired word of God.

More formally:

The Bible says God exists.
The Bible is the inspired word of God (or, was written by God).
Therefore, God exists.

The second premise assumes that God exists, since he could not have inspired the Bible if he did not exist. Yet that statement ("God exists") is exactly the conclusion that the argument is trying to prove.

Consider these two examples as well:

Nothing tastes better than chocolate ice cream, since every other food is inferior in taste.
We all have the same rights. Therefore, everyone is equal.

The premise in each assumes the truth of the conclusion it tries to prove. So, each argument commits the fallacy of begging the question.

Non sequitur ("that which does not follow"). A non sequitur is the logical fallacy of drawing a conclusion from a premise or premises that are irrelevant to the conclusion, that provide no support for the conclusion. Consider this simple example:

All men are mortal.
Socrates is a man.
Therefore, Socrates is bald.

The premises say nothing about whether all or some men are bald, and so cannot prove the conclusion that Socrates is bald. They are irrelevant to the conclusion and the inference from them to the conclusion is a non sequitur.

Here is a timelier example:

Politician: There is nothing more important than the public heath of this community. Therefore, every citizen in town should get vaccinated for smallpox twice a year.

The premise is not relevant to the conclusion because the premise does not establish that (a) smallpox is a public health problem in that community and (b) if smallpox is a public health problem, that two vaccinations a year are necessary to solve the problem (maybe only one vaccination in a lifetime is needed) or sufficient to solve the problem (maybe five vaccinations are required).

Here is a non sequitur in the form of an old joke:

One college student to another: I will never, ever, ever get drunk on alcohol, because my cousin Joe did once and now he is living in Arkansas.

Drinking alcohol to excess does not have any (causal) connection to where one lives, and so the premise does not support the conclusion that if the speaker were to get drunk he also would be living in Arkansas.

Non sequiturs are more common than you may think, especially in public discourse about politics, policy issues, and social problems. Consider this final example:

One voter to another: Of course you should vote for candidate X. She is very attractive.

To put the argument a bit more formally:

Candidate X is very attractive.
Therefore, you (all voters) should vote for X.

Being physically attractive is a great asset if you are an actor like Jennifer Lopez or Brad Pitt. But presumably we want our political leaders to have other traits, like being able to work with other people, having good policy ideas, not being corrupt, and so on. Candidate X's physical appearance is not a relevant reason to vote for her. (If you think it is, would you still have that view if her policy ideas are terrible or silly and she was found guilty of ten acts of bribery and public corruption?)

Finally, sometimes it is difficult to distinguish between a non sequitur and an enthymatic argument. Recall this argument from chapter 7:

There's absolutely no way to determine that the person being punished, or
the person against whom revenge is taken, was capable of behaving differently from the way they behaved.
Therefore, punishment and revenge are unjust.

You might consider this a non sequitur because the premise says nothing about what is just or unjust, and so it does not establish the conclusion. But the premise is not obviously irrelevant to the conclusion. Both the premise and the conclusion talk about punishment and revenge, and the premise could be made relevant to the conclusion with an additional premise, as we saw in our earlier discussion when we added an implied general rule as the first premise:

It is always unjust to punish a person or to inflict revenge on a person if (1) that person committed an illegal (or immoral) act and (2) we cannot determine that they could have done otherwise.
There's absolutely no way to determine that the person being punished, or the person against whom revenge is taken, was capable of behaving differently from the way they behaved.
Therefore, punishment and revenge are unjust.

So, a better reading of this argument is that it is an enthymeme. (Recall our discussion of enthymemes in chapter 4.) You may sound rather foolish if you criticize an author or speaker for making an argument that is a non sequitur when she is only doing what is commonly done, namely, assuming that a premise is so well known or so widely accepted that it need not be expressly stated.

Ad hominem (literally, "directed to the man"). This fallacy has several forms. In one form, the person making a fallacious ad hominem argument attacks the person making an argument rather than attacking the premises of that argument. Consider these examples of this form of ad hominem argument:

The American State Department shouldn't criticize my country's record on human rights. America violates the human rights of its own citizens every day.
You argue that global warming is not caused by humans' burning fossil fuels because you're the president of a large oil company.

As indicated by these examples, and the ones that follow, the ad hominem fallacy is, unfortunately, found in much political discussion.

In its second form, an ad hominem argument appeals to the listener's special circumstances as a ground for accepting or rejecting the speaker's conclusion, rather than supporting that conclusion with reasons any person could accept. For example:

> Of course you should support my antiabortion position, you're a Catholic. You won't believe anything our scientists say about climate change because you, Senator, get lots of contributions from the oil industry.

Ignorance. Arguments committing the fallacy of ignorance argue either that some statement is true because no one has ever proven it to be false or that some statement is false because it has not been proven to be true.

> I believe in unicorns because no one has ever proven that they do not exist.

More formally:

> No one has ever proven that unicorns do not exist.
> Therefore, (I believe that) unicorns exist.

Consider this common argument in the context of the debate over evolution and intelligent design:

> The theory of evolution is just speculation, not truth. Because no one has ever proven it to be true.

An argument asserts that some fact or opinion stated in a premise is true (e.g., All men are mortal). Ignorance is the absence of knowledge of or the absence of a belief in the truth of a fact or opinion. No conclusion can logically follow from a statement of the absence of knowledge or belief. Even the prevalence of ignorance does not make it a rational basis for drawing any conclusions.

When an argument seems to go astray, ask yourself, "has the author committed a fallacy of some sort?" Often, you will find that he has. Educating yourself to the many types of fallacies can be a lot of fun, especially since so many jokes are the products of some form of fallacy. You can find many additional examples of the fallacies discussed here and other fallacies on the internet and in many published logic texts. Reading these sources will be worth your time.

NECESSARY AND SUFFICIENT CONDITIONS

You can go through years of higher education and never be taught the difference between a necessary condition and a sufficient condition, or even hear from any of your teachers that there is such a thing as a necessary condition or a sufficient condition. That is unfortunate. You will be intellectually poorer for this omission. So many of the debates you will hear in your favorite bar, in the media, in academics, or across the family table on Thanksgiving Day are mired in confusion because the author's or speaker's intellectual commitments are not clear.

A quick example will illustrate its importance.

> Corruption will continue in Washington politics until the people defeat the politicians through the ballot box.

This statement may be read in two different ways. First, it may mean that if the people defeat the politicians through the ballot box, such defeats *alone* are sufficient to eliminate corruption; it leaves unanswered whether such defeats are necessary to eliminate corruption. Second, it may mean that such defeats are necessary to eliminating corruption; it leaves open whether other steps are also necessary or whether defeats alone are necessary. The second reading takes such defeats to be a necessary condition of solving the problem, but not necessarily the entire solution, not necessarily a sufficient condition. If a pundit on TV or in an opinion piece were to make this statement without further explanation, you could not know which reading he intends. Sometimes that ambiguity is intentional; sometimes it reflects sloppy thinking.

NECESSARY CONDITIONS

To say that Y is a necessary condition of X is to say that the truth of Y is necessary for X to be true. A few simple examples will illustrate this. Suppose you own a regular, standard gas-fueled (not electric) car. You are talking to a friend and tell her:

> I can drive my car to Dubuque only if it has gas in it.

And what you are saying, from a logical point of view, is:

> "My car has gas in it" being true is a necessary condition for "my driving my car to Dubuque" to be true.

Or, more colloquially:

It is a necessary condition for my driving my car to Dubuque that it have gas in it.

This can be rephrased, once again, as:

If there's no gas in the car, I can't drive it to Dubuque.

No matter how it is phrased, you are saying that there is no way that "my driving to Dubuque" can be true if "having gas in the car" is false.

Let's try another example. Suppose you instead say to your friend, "Only if my car is painted red, can I drive it to Dubuque." Your statement can be rephrased as:

I can drive my car to Dubuque only if it is painted red.

And what you are saying, from a logical point of view, is:

My car being painted red is a necessary condition for my driving it to Dubuque.

Or:

It is a necessary condition for my driving my car to Dubuque that it be painted red.

This can be rephrased, once again, as:

If my car is not painted red, then I can't drive it to Dubuque.

No matter how it is phrased, you are saying that the truth of "having the car painted red" is a *necessary* condition of the truth of "my driving it to Dubuque."

Now, assuming a normal state of affairs when you make these statements, you are correct that having gas in the car is a necessary condition of driving it to Dubuque (or anywhere else), and wrong when you say having it painted red is a necessary condition of driving it to Dubuque. (Plenty of cars drive to Dubuque whether they are painted red, green, black, white, or any combination of colors.) The point is that in a lot of arguments, we often hear people say that some thing is a necessary condition of some other thing, and it may or may not be.

Gas in the tank of a car and its paint color are not the stuff of many arguments or debates, public or private. So, let's look at an example that you may read in an editorial piece or hear from an activist or politician:

The only way to stop global warming is to eliminate the use of fossil fuels.

How would you rephrase that statement in terms of a necessary condition? It would be something like this:

Eliminating the use of fossil fuels is a necessary condition of stopping global warming.

Or, alternatively, and equally good:

Global warming will stop (or, We can stop global warming) only if we eliminate the use of fossil fuels.

We are not going to debate here whether the statement is right or wrong, but we are going to try to understand it and its implications.

Most importantly, in saying that the elimination of fossil fuels is a necessary condition of stopping global warming, the speaker is in effect saying that we can do any number of other things (e.g., plant 500 million trees, drive solar-powered electric cars, become vegetarians, capture and store carbon, cut the use of fossil fuels by 50 percent, and so on), and that none of them individually or in any combination will stop global warming. Why? Because this speaker believes that the truth of "the *elimination* of the use of fossil fuels" is *necessary* for the truth of "global warming will stop." Now, whether that is true or false, it is a strong statement, one that in any rational debate the speaker would need to prove. And if it is proven, it may have important consequences for any laws or public policy adopted to deal with global warming.

We will come back to this example in our discussion of sufficient conditions. Before we do that, review the examples above. Do you see any words in those examples that are red flags of necessary conditions? Keep these in mind. *Also keep in mind, however, that these are only signals, and not every usage of one of these templates is a foolproof guide to a necessary condition.* There is no substitute for thinking through what an author is trying to communicate.

- "Only if." When you see this phrase the speaker generally is saying that whatever follows "only if" is a necessary condition. The "car having gas in it" is a necessary condition, and "the elimination of fossil fuels" is a necessary condition, and they both follow "only if."

- "If . . ., then . . ." When you see "if X, then Y," whatever stands in the place of the "Y" is typically said to be a necessary condition. In our two previous examples—"If I can drive to Dubuque, then the car has gas in it" and "If we are to stop global warming, then we must eliminate the use of fossil fuels"—everything following "then" is said to be a necessary condition.
- "If not . . ., then not . . ." When you see "if not X, then not Y," whatever stands in the place of X usually is said to be a necessary condition of Y. In other words, whenever you see this template, you can flip the X and Y, and eliminate the "not" in both parts, and the X will be the necessary condition of Y. In two of our previous examples—(a) "If there's no gas in the car, I can't drive it to Dubuque" and (b) "If the car is not painted red, then I can't drive it to Dubuque"—can be rewritten as (a) "If I can drive it to Dubuque, then there's gas in the car" and (b) "If I can drive it to Dubuque, then the car is painted red," and in both cases, the parts following "then" are said to be necessary conditions of driving the car to Dubuque.

Remember, these are only tips, general guidelines, not hard and fast rules. What you read is sometimes ambiguous and does not always conform to simple rules.

A word of caution before we proceed. To say that X is a necessary condition of Y is to make a point about the logical relationship of X and Y, not a point about causes and effects in the world. If Anne states, "If I can drive my car to Dubuque, then it is painted red," she is not stating that having it painted red is an effect (or a cause) of her driving it to Dubuque. Rather, she is stating the logical point that, *if* "I can drive my car to Dubuque" is true, then it is necessary that "it is painted red" is true. If this is not entirely clear, keep this point in mind as we discuss other examples, and it will become clearer.

SUFFICIENT CONDITIONS

To say that X is a sufficient condition of Y is to say that the truth of X is all that is needed (is sufficient) for Y to be true. Let's begin to discuss sufficient conditions with our driving example.

If I am driving to Dubuque, then there is gas in the car.

The phrase "I am driving to Dubuque" is the sufficient condition. The statement is saying that if "I am driving to Dubuque" is true, then that is sufficient for "there is gas in the car" to be true.

Let's flip the sentence around:

If there is gas in the car, then I am driving to Dubuque.

Here, the truth of "there is gas in the car" is *said* to be the sufficient condition for the truth of "I am driving to Dubuque." And it may be, given the right context. Suppose Joe is trying to make a decision as to whether to drive to Dubuque, but he is a bit low on cash. If he were to make this statement, then what he may be saying is that, "the truth of 'there is gas in the car' is all that I need (a sufficient condition) for me to make (to decide) 'I am driving to Dubuque' true." Of course, you can imagine many other circumstances when having gas in the car is not really a sufficient condition, even though someone says it is. There could be gas in the car and I am not driving it at all because, for example, it has four flat tires or because I am driving it somewhere other than Dubuque. So, the sentence *says* that the truth of "having gas in the car" is sufficient for "I am driving it to Dubuque" to be true, but the sufficient condition could be true or false.

Let's try a variation on our fossil fuels example.

If we eliminate the use of fossil fuels, then we will stop global warming.

Or, equivalently:

Eliminating the use of fossil fuels is sufficient to stop global warming.

Here, "we eliminate the use of fossil fuels" is said to be the sufficient condition of "stop global warming." What is the speaker saying when she makes such a statement? She is saying that *all we need to do* to stop global warming is to stop using fossil fuels. Nothing more than that—that is sufficient. More precisely, she is saying that if "we eliminate the use of fossil fuels" is true, then that is sufficient for "we will stop global warming" to be true.

Again, we are not going to debate whether that is a true or false statement. But we do want to ask, what is the speaker committing to when she makes such a statement? She is committing to at least the following positions: (1) that we could burn any other kind of fuel (e.g., wood and biofuels) or use any other kind of fuel (e.g., solar energy or wind power) and, nonetheless, if we eliminate fossil fuel use, we would eliminate global warming and (2) any other measures we are now taking or may take to address global warming are unnecessary as long as we eliminate the use of fossil fuels.

Note that here—unlike in our discussion of necessary conditions—the speaker is *not* saying that eliminating the use of fossil fuels is necessary to stop global warming; she is not stating all of the actions necessary to stop global warming. She is just saying that this one step is a sufficient measure to achieve this goal.

This last point may have you scratching your head. If it is sufficient that we eliminate the use of fossil fuels to stop global warming, then why is that not a necessary condition also? Because eliminating fossil fuels may be just one of many options and not a necessary course of action, not a necessary condition. Suppose the author knows of a technology to neutralize all of the bad effects of continuing to use fossil fuels so that this continued use did not contribute to global warming. Then, the truth of "eliminating the use of fossil fuels" would not be necessary to the truth of "stopping global warming." Their continued use would not make any more difference with respect to global warming than whether you wore red or blue pants on Tuesday. So, eliminating their use can be a sufficient but not a necessary condition of stopping global warming.

More generally, depending on what you are talking about, something can be a sufficient condition and not also be a necessary condition, and something can be a necessary condition without also being a sufficient condition. And some things are not either necessary or sufficient conditions. And, finally, something may be both a necessary and sufficient condition.

Recall our example on eating more fiber, discussed in chapter 4. Suppose you read an article that began like this:

If you want to eat something for better heath, you ought to eat fiber.

How would you restate this in terms of a sufficient condition? Like this:

Eating food with fiber is sufficient for producing better health.

Or, alternatively,

If you eat food with fiber, then you will have better health.

The author is stating that the truth of "(you) eating foods with fiber" is enough by itself to make "you will have better health" true. She is not stating that this is necessary to your having better health, since she is not excluding the possibility that eating foods without fiber but with lots of vitamins, fish oil, or minerals may also produce better health. She just does not speak to whether any one type of food, or all of the types of foods, that may be necessary to produce better health.

Here is one final example of sufficient conditions.

> Question (from a reporter): How can we produce widespread prosperity in this country?

Answer (from a politician): All we need to do is to break up the concentration of wealth and economic power of corporations.

The politician is stating that the truth of "breaking up the concentration of wealth and economic power of corporations" is by itself (is sufficient) for the truth of "producing widespread prosperity."

What are the red flags that point to sufficient conditions? What are the helpful tips to keep in mind? As with necessary conditions, you need to think through what the author is trying to communicate.

- "If X, then Y." When you see this template, the X usually states the sufficient condition.
- "X only if Y." Again, X typically states the sufficient condition.
- "Only if Y, then X." This can be restated as "X only if Y," or as "If X, then Y." We know that, generally, Y is the necessary condition and that means that X states the sufficient condition.
- "If not X, then not Y." For example, "if it's not sunny, then we're not in San Diego." Whenever you see this template, you can flip the X and Y, and eliminate the "not" in both parts, and the Y usually will be the sufficient condition of X. To continue the example, in "if we're in San Diego, then it's sunny," the truth of "we're in San Diego" is said to be sufficient for the truth of "it's sunny." (Recall that we did a similar sort of switching and eliminating the negative in our discussion of necessary conditions. See page 129.)

Remember, these are only signals, general guidelines, not hard and fast rules that some phrase is a sufficient condition. What you read is sometimes ambiguous and does not always conform to simple rules.

It is useful to echo the word of caution stated at the end of our discussion of necessary conditions. To say that X is a sufficient condition of Y is to make a point about the logical relationship of X and Y, not a point about causes and effects in the world. If Kathy states, "If I can drive my car to Dubuque, then it is painted red," she is not stating that driving it to Dubuque is a cause (or effect) of it being painted red. Rather, she is stating the logical point that, *if* "I can drive my car to Dubuque" is true, then that is sufficient for "it is painted red" to be true.

The more logic you know, the better you will be at analyzing the arguments in argumentative texts. As the previous chapters of this book demonstrate, logic alone is not sufficient to understand what a text or an argument in a text means. It is not even necessary to understanding what a text or an argument means. It is, however, a necessary part of forming a judgment as to whether an argument is valid or invalid, or strong or weak. Accordingly, in reading for understanding, you will benefit from further study of logic through sources beyond this book.

Chapter 10

Conclusion

My alma mater was books, a good library. Every time I catch a plane, I have with me a book that I want to read—and that's a lot of books these days.—Malcolm X, *Autobiography of Malcolm X*, p. 183

The tools we have discussed in this book are not going to change your life dramatically and swiftly. They are not the equivalent of a magic wand that you wave to leave a black-and-white world and enter into a world full of thousands of vibrant colors. But they may change your life step-by-step. An athlete, artist, cook, doctor, and furniture maker each gets better at his or her craft over time, with each new effort they put into mastering their arts. Analyzing and reading argumentative texts is no different. And the rewards are *at least* equally great.

Being a better reader of argumentative texts leads to a more meaningful life, a deeper understanding of oneself, others, and the social and political world we inhabit. Accordingly, it fosters a greater ability to engage with that world in productive and satisfying ways. Greater understanding is good in and of itself, and it has the additional benefit of being empowering.

The previous chapters have given you a lot to think about and to work through. We have discussed many tools for making you a better reader of argumentative texts, for giving you a better understanding of what those texts mean or may mean. Specifically, the tools we have discussed include: distinguishing argumentative from nonargumentative texts; knowing the major types of arguments (deductive, inductive, theoretical, practical); the analysis of a text's structure (introductions, outlines, and summaries); the analysis of ambiguous terms, phrases, and sentences; recognizing types of statements other than factual, literal statements (normative, ironical, and rhetorical statements); the importance of context; and, knowing common errors in reasoning and the importance of necessary and sufficient conditions.

In addition, we discussed at various places in this book what you are doing, or beneficially could be doing, when you are trying to understand a difficult argumentative work. More particularly, we discussed the importance of using an initial critical reaction as a first step to a better understanding of what the author is trying to communicate, her meaning. We can all spend a lot of energy talking past each other with little understanding of each other. Yet ask yourself, could there be a more productive and satisfying use of our intellects? This book has given you the tools to answer this question with a strong "yes." The companion *Workbook for Reading Argumentative Texts* includes many exercises and case studies that allow you to sharpen these tools and to learn a few new ones.

At several places, this book stresses that there is no one authoritative reading of any text. Rather, there are four guideposts at the outer limits of any reading, and if you cross any one of them, your reading has little claim to being a "good" reading. These are worth your review and repeated study (see chapter 3, where we first discussed them). Presumably you have learned a lot more in this book than these four points, of course. But if you keep these guideposts in mind, they can prove very useful once you have put this book down and are wrestling with a text on your own.

I wish you the best of luck in your lifelong education, and I hope you have many days of better reading ahead.

> *What an astonishing thing a* book *is . . . one glance at it and you're inside the mind of another person, maybe somebody dead for thousands of years. Across the millennia, an author is speaking clearly and silently inside your head, directly to you. Books break the shackles of time. A book is proof that humans are capable of working magic.*—Carl Sagan (American astronomer, cosmologist, and author, 1934–1996), in *Cosmos: A Personal Voyage*, episode 11 (1990) (a television series)

Appendix A: Study Latin If You Want to Talk Like a Supervillain

Frankie Thomas

Published as an oral essay on the PBS NewsHour, April 11, 2018; transcript available at, Opinion: Study Latin If You Want to Talk Like a Supervillain | PBS NewsHour.

If you can possibly get away with it, you should study Latin.

Okay, hear me out. Yes, any modern language offers more practical benefits than Latin. But Latin offers more fun. It has all the pleasures of a puzzle, a time capsule, and a secret code. You say dead language; I say ghost-hunting.

My favorite thing about Latin is that all of its native speakers are dead. You'll never have to talk to them! This makes Latin the perfect subject for introverts. There's no pressure to become conversationally fluent, and no Latin teacher will ever force you to turn to your classmate and have an awkward scripted conversation about your winter break.

In fact, Latin doesn't even have the vocabulary for discussing your winter break—or anything else going on in your boring life. Unlike beginner Spanish or French—which teaches you to say, "I would like a salad" and "Where is the library?"—beginner Latin teaches you to talk like a supervillain. Wheelock's Latin, the standard beginner textbook at the college level, teaches you how to say the following sentences:

"You are all to blame, and tomorrow you will pay the ultimate price."
"Our army is great, and because of the number of our arrows, you shall not see the sky."
"Human life is punishment."

How can you not love a language that immerses you in this epic world of war and gods and gladiators, where every sentence is fraught with portent and someone is usually about to get murdered? My middle school Latin textbook had a passage about a barber—pretty tame, right?—a barber who accidentally cuts his customer's throat. To this day, we all remember how to say *multus sanguis fluit*: "Much blood flows."

That barber, by the way, was a real guy; he lived in Pompeii, as did all the characters in that textbook. Here are some other vocab words it taught us: volcano. To erupt. Ashes. To be in despair. Did I mention that all native Latin speakers are dead? Not only that, but many of them died horribly—buried alive in volcanic ash—which is why we know so much about them today. To study Latin is to engage with the dead.

True, you can't talk to them directly—and thank the gods for that, because what would we talk about? Winter break?

But they have a way of getting into your head, with their beautiful useless words. No one speaks Latin anymore, no one needs Latin anymore . . . and yet here we are. Here I am, watching my favorite sitcom, mentally translating the dialogue—*Noli, Deandra dulcis, meretrix ebria et pugnax esse!*—and remembering that nothing is permanent. Not emperors. Not gods. Not even me.

So that's how studying Latin will change your life. You might never get a chance to use what you've learned. But it will live in your memory forever. And in that sense—here's the secret of Latin—it's not really a dead language at all.

Appendix B: Ayanna Pressley Is Right: 16-Year-Olds Deserve the Right to Vote

Nancy Deutsch

Originally published in Newsweek, November 1, 2019, and available at newsweek. com/ayanna-pressley-right-16-year-olds-deserve-right-vote-opinion-1469043

For our democracy to function as it should, we need to encourage more Americans—from diverse racial and socioeconomic backgrounds and age groups—to vote in local and federal elections.

This imperative is front and center as we approach another Election Day here in Virginia and across the country.

Over the course of our 400-year history, we have seen a greater number of individuals access this fundamental right, advancing our nation further and further toward the ideal set forth by our founders. Yet, in recent years, much has been made of the apparent fragility of American representative democracy. Pundits and armchair commentators of all political persuasions complain about notoriously low voter turnout, decrying large segments of the voting public as apathetic, uninformed or even illegitimate.

Still, relatively few organizations and legislators have recommended the bold solutions needed to increase the representativeness of our electorate.

Perhaps the most compelling idea, and the most democratic in spirit, is a 2018 proposal, from U.S. Representative Ayanna Pressley of Massachusetts, to lower the voting age in federal elections to 16. Unsurprisingly, Pressley's amendment to a voting rights bill fell flat on the House floor.

Setting aside legislators' risk-averse decision-making and political calculations, the consensus was that 16-year-olds cannot reasonably contribute to the electoral process.

Even though 16 is the age when many teens can realize the rights and responsibilities of adulthood (such as driving and full employment), we say they somehow lack the maturity and experience to make informed choices at the ballot box. Opponents of the idea argue that 16-year-olds will just vote the same way their parents do.

The thing is, we don't really have a good reason not to allow 16-year-olds to vote. In fact, the evidence suggests just the opposite—that enfranchising 16-year-olds would be good for them and good for our democracy.

The skeptical attitude toward the next generation is especially baffling when we see teens like Greta Thunberg, or the students from Parkland, Florida, consistently demonstrate independent thought, deep understanding, clear convictions, and tremendous maturity and poise in the national and international limelight (even amid jarring criticism and judgment from adults).

These exceptional young people are far more informed than the average adult when it comes to key issues of our time and, of course, are far more engaged than many of their peers. Never mind that the claims about young people being ill-informed and inexperienced essentially reprise the same complaints that were made when women and African Americans sought suffrage. Never mind the fact that a fair number of 16-year-olds are taxpayers who have no say in the election of the officials who determine how their tax dollars are spent. Never mind that the decisions those officials make are affecting the day-to-day lives of 16-year-olds today. In fact, these 16-year-olds will be living with the consequences of those decisions for far longer than today's lawmakers and vast majority of the current electorate.

Science tells us that adolescents are primed to demonstrate the level of engagement we hope to see in the voting public. A recent report from the National Academies of Science, Engineering and Medicine shows that adolescents have an increased capacity to exhibit complex reasoning, strategic problem-solving skills and use of evidence to make significant decisions. Adolescents also have a higher tolerance for ambiguity and risk, both of which are essential to participating, and engaging, in a healthy electoral process and discourse.

We know from this same research that there is no better way to promote sustained civic engagement than to nurture it earlier in our teens' lives. The adolescent years represent a critical period of identity formation, presenting us with an opportunity to ensure a new generation of voters see themselves as engaged participants in our democracy.

At the same time, the adolescent brain is actively making new neural connections, meaning that habits formed during these years can be long lasting. Imagine the positive impact on our society if voting was a habit for the next generation.

Appendix B: Ayanna Pressley Is Right: 16-Year-Olds Deserve the Right to Vote 141

Some communities have already had success in trusting the potential of our adolescents—and thereby increasing voter turnout and representation—by lowering the voting age to 16 in their local elections. Takoma Park, Maryland, for example, extended the right to vote to 16- and 17-year-olds in 2013. Over the ensuing six years, the city saw a voter turnout rate among this age group that nearly doubled that of the electorate age 18 and older.

The notion that adolescents are incapable of exercising the sober judgment needed to place a vote reflects a broader, misguided prejudice against young people that prevents initiatives like the one in Takoma Park from taking root in jurisdictions across the country. This prejudice is not a sound basis for continuing to deny adolescents a say in our democracy—and constraining the promise of our representative democracy for years to come.

It is time to enfranchise our 16-year-olds.

Index

ambiguity. *See* ambiguous
ambiguous: defined, 10, 94; semantic, 94–95; syntactic, 94–95
analogy, reasoning by, 38, 43–44, 52n5, 103–4; as a form of inductive argument, 38, 43–44
Anthony, Susan B., 68–69
antidotes for fear, 62–63, 65–66, 108
argument: deductive, 36–37, 39; defined, 2, 7, 31; four types of, 39, *39*; inductive, 37–38; invalid, 39–41; practical, 6, 13n1, 76; strong, 42–44; theoretical, 6, 13n1, 77; valid, 39–41; weak, 42–44
Aristotle, 34, 49, 53, 71n1, 112

Birmingham jail, 107–8, 113, 116
Booth, Wayne C., 29n1

causal explanation. *See* explanation, casual
conditional statement, 76
conditions, 11, 126–33; necessary, 126–29; sufficient, 129–32
context, 10–11, 19, 111–18; as a source of meaning, 10–11, 112; cultural, 115–17; intellectual, 112–15; physical, 117–18; political, 115–17; social, 115–17. *See also* meaning

descriptive writing, 47–48
Deutsch, Nancy, 84–85, 139

Edmundson, Mark, 26
Emerson, Ralph Waldo, 12
enthymematic argument. *See* enthymeme
enthymeme, 44–45, 81, 98, 123–24; defined, 44
explanation, causal, 48–49
explanatory writing, 48–49, 51
expository writing, 46–47

factual statements, 96
fallacy, 119–25; *ad hominem*, 124–25; begging the question (circular reasoning), 121–22; defined, 119; equivocation, 119–21; ignorance, 125; *non sequitur*, 122–24
Feinberg, Joel, 62, 65
Freud, Sigmund, 58

Gardner, John W., 59
Gross, Hyman, 63–64

Hume, David, 98

implied premise. *See* enthymeme

143

information, reading for: defined, 27.
    See also reading
in medias res, 111
introductions, 53–72; anecdotal, 66–68;
    asking a question (stating a problem),
    62–66, 84–85; just the facts, ma'am,
    just the facts, 69–70; let's get right to
    the point, 68–69; Road Map, 54–59;
    Subject Variation, 59–61
irony, 10, 93, 106–7, 110n3;
    defined, 106

Kennedy, John F., 50
King, Dr. Martin Luther, Jr., 62–63,
    107–8, 113, 116
Kooser, Ted, 9

Latin, article on studying, 74–81,
    97–98, 137–38
Lincoln, Abraham, 115–16
logic, 119–33; logical connections as
    a source of meaning, 11. *See also*
    fallacy; conditional statement;
    conditions

Malcolm X, 12
meaning: defined, 7, 10; not found
    solely in the statements that
    constitute the argument, 7, 24;
    principal sources of, 10–11
Mill, John Stuart, 60–61, 114

necessary condition. *See* conditions
normative statement, 10, 93, 96–106

op-ed, defined, 92n1

Plato, 62, 65, 66
premise, 2, 7, 31

reading: as a dialogue, 16–21; not a
    spectator sport, 15–16; to become
    wise, 28–29; to obtain information,
    27–28; to understand, 23–27
reasonableness, zone of. *See* zone of
    reasonableness
rhetoric, 5, 10, 94, 107–9; defined, 49
rhetorical writing, 49–51
Richards, David A. J., 57

Shawn, Wallace, 99–102
Staples, Brent A., 108–9
state of affairs, 33
straw man, 91
straw woman, 91
structure of a text: as a source of
    meaning, 10, 73. *See also* meaning
sufficient condition. *See* conditions
surrogacy, 102–5

text: argumentative, 7–8; defined, 7
thesis, 2, 7, 31, 55, 61
Thomas, Frankie, 137
truth, 40–41

understanding, reading for: as a
    dialogue, 16–21; should precede and
    aid critical judgment, 26–27, 136.
    See also reading

voting rights, 68–69, 82; article
    on lowering the voting age,
    82–88, 139–41

wisdom: defined, 28
wise, reading to become. *See* reading

zone of reasonableness, 24–27, 109

About the Author

James E. Scheuermann received his B.A. (in history) and his Ph.D. (in philosophy) from the University of Chicago. He received his J.D. from the University of Pittsburgh School of Law. He is a former high school and college teacher and for more than thirty years has been a practicing lawyer with a major international law firm. He is the author of numerous articles in scholarly philosophy journals and law reviews, and in other legal publications.

www.ingramcontent.com/pod-product-compliance
Lightning Source LLC
Chambersburg PA
CBHW022015300426
44117CB00005B/197